CRYPTOCURRENCY AND REAL ESTATE

HOW TO PROFIT AS BITCOIN AND BLOCKCHAIN REVOLUTIONIZE REAL ESTATE INVESTING

Steve Streetman

CRYPTOCURRENCY AND REAL ESTATE

Steve Streetman

DEDICATION

O VER THE YEARS, I have had the great privilege of being associated with several groups of real estate investors. I have learned much from each of those groups, and I have grown as an investor with each encounter. Many people have taken the time to teach me, not just during classes, but as we have structured deals together. I would like to dedicate this book to the professionals who have furthered my own investing career. I hope to pay that forward at least partially through the vehicle of this book. I would like to particularly mention Dave Lindahl and the RE Mentor Group, Sherman Ragland and Realinvestors®, and Gene Guarino and RAL Academy. They have all helped me. Sherman, in particular, I credit with the idea of writing a book to share what I know.

But the group that brought the two disciplines of cryptocurrency and real estate together for me and helped me understand the Reese's Cup of investing is the National Council of Exchangors (NCE) and especially my mentor and friend Bob Steele. This book would not be possible without all I have learned at the NCE meetings as this incredibly talented group of real estate brokers discuss deal structures that would make most brokers' heads explode. You guys rock.

CONTENTS

PREFACE

I N 2017, I WAS approached by a broker who later became my friend and mentor, Robert (Bob) Steele. He offered me cryptocurrency in exchange for land I was trying to help someone sell. I had heard of Bitcoin, of course, but had no idea of the emerging world of cryptocurrency. I did my due diligence and investigated the cryptocurrency. What I found was a whole ecosystem of emerging financial technology ideas, technology, and business approaches. It was exhilarating. It was challenging to put the deal—a three-way exchange—together. I had to find new ways of understanding the relationship between real estate, cryptocurrency, lending, and fiat currency. But I persisted, and we closed in October of 2017.

From that start, a substantial exchange of real estate for cryptocurrency, I entered the world of crypto full-bore. Over the past few years, I have learned loads about my two investing passions, cryptocurrency and real estate. I had already been a real estate investor since 2004, and I met Bob through an extremely creative group of real estate investors and brokers, the National Council of Exchangors (NCE) (https://ncexchangors.com). The wide range of strategies they advocate in their approach to solving real estate problems for sellers and buyers have informed my own approach to investing. And I am greatly indebted to the professionals I have met through the NCE for their investing advice and collective wisdom.

The challenges I have faced in completing crypto transactions were often a surprise to me, but through persistence, collaboration, and more than a little creativity, I have closed some transactions and am poised to close others. Items like title insurance or a 75% loan to value loan that real estate investors take for granted can become an almost insurmountable obstacle when cryptocurrency is in the mix. In this book, I describe the techniques I used and the issues I have come across. You won't have to recreate the methods as I did. You are getting the benefit of my experience so you can avoid the same pitfalls.

As an investor who relishes finding creative approaches to real estate problems, I have devoured everything I could find on the intersection of real estate and cryptocurrency. Unfortunately, there just isn't that much out there. The two worlds don't seem to intersect much—not nearly as much as they should—beyond vague ideas of putting real estate on the blockchain. And when I did find people working at the intersection of real estate and crypto, they seemed to be narrowly focused on one idea. The genesis of this book was a desire for a more thorough treatment of the synergies between real estate and cryptocurrency. I think you will find that some of the concepts in this book appear nowhere else. The discussion of barter currency is one. The ideas for loyalty programs for real estate businesses using utility tokens is another. Those topics that are discussed elsewhere (like security tokens or real estate title on the blockchain) I've embedded in a broader framework of crypto and real estate that can form a basis for new ways of combining the two. That framework—transforming deal-making, transforming ownership, and transforming management—consolidates disparate topics into actionable knowledge for investors.

Please take everything in this book as food for thought. Cryptocurrency redefines the term 'rapidly evolving'. I have tried to make everything in the book accurate as of the writing, but so much changes so fast that it is impossible to ensure that everything is still accurate by the time you are reading it. These concerns are especially relevant when it comes to the tax advantages and consequences of cryptocurrency for real estate deals. I am not a lawyer. I am not an accountant. Before you make an investment decision, consult a competent professional yourself. Lastly, I will only be discussing U.S. tax implications. I imagine many countries will follow a similar treatment, but you should check.

Because cryptocurrency evolves so rapidly, you may want additional resources that are kept up to date. I am working hard to provide those resources and make them available to interested parties. You can get access by contacting me or by going to the CryptoREBook.com site below.

I am incredibly excited to see how the relationship between cryptocurrency and real estate matures over the next few years. It's going to be a wild ride, but those who learn the principles of how crypto and real estate interact will be poised to take full advantage of the combination. Cryptocurrency has made more billionaires in less time than any other asset class. Real estate has always been the tried and true way to create wealth; even those who made their money in other fields originally preserved and grew their wealth through real estate. The nexus between them is a recipe for turbo-charged investing.

Because cryptocurrency is so new, there is a lot of misinformation about it on the internet. I have tried to weed through the wild claims and get to the truth. To the extent that I have failed, the responsibility is mine. If there are later editions of this book, I will correct anything I find is wrong and update what has changed.

I want to thank my editor, Susan Gaigher. She has been a joy to work with and has been very good at finding my flaws and gently correcting them. We have collaborated completely remotely (thank you, Covid-19). I hope to actually meet her one day and thank her again in person.

If you are anywhere near as interested in this topic as I am, please connect with me beyond the words on these pages. My contact info is below. The best way to reach me is through the CryptoREBook site. We can start a collaboration together to transform real estate investing with cryptocurrency.

Phone: 301-332-3750
Email: steve@streetsmartinvestmentsllc.com
Websites: go to my website, https://StreetSmartInvestmentsLLC.com for investment information and to https://CryptoREBook.com for additional materials related to the book and the topic of cryptocurrency and real estate.

USEFUL TERMINOLOGY

A LL TERMS ARE DEFINED in the book where they arise, but for ease of reference, below is a compendium of cryptocurrency and real estate terms.

Appreciation: increase in value of an asset over time. Appreciation may be driven by changes in the market or may be forced by improving the underlying asset.

Barter currency/Barter cryptocurrency: a unique type of cryptocurrency focused on trading for assets rather than exchanging on a cryptocurrency exchange. The first barter currency was TROPTIONS, but there are several related tokens currently available.

Basis: the cost of acquiring and/or developing an asset. The basis is used as your original cost of an asset when assessing taxable gains.

Bitcoin: the original and most popular cryptocurrency. It has by far the greatest market value and the best liquidity of any cryptocurrency.

Blockchain: a growing list of records, called blocks, that are linked using cryptography. Each block contains a cryptographic hash of the previous block, a timestamp, and transaction data. The blockchain is where records of cryptocurrency transactions are stored. When properly implemented and independently maintained, the records on the blockchain are immutable.

Cashflow/Cash-on-cash return: a type of return from an asset that represents the actual cash received within a year. Cashflow is usually measured as the amount of net cash divided by the original investment amount. When calculated this way, it is also called the cash-on-cash return.

Control: for the purposes of this book, the method by which an investor 'owns' an asset. Types of control are through a deed (also known as fee simple control), a lease, an option, or a contract.

Cryptocurrency/Crypto/Crypto asset: a digital asset designed to work as a medium of exchange that uses cryptography to secure its transactions, to control the creation of additional units, and to verify the transfer of assets.

Crypto exchange: a website where cryptocurrency can be exchanged for other cryptocurrency or for fiat currency. In the future there may be exchanges where cryptocurrency can be exchanged for other products or assets.

Debt: refers to loans that are secured by an asset and must be repaid to a lender.

Depreciation: a tax concept where the cost of an asset is deducted from income over time. Depreciation refers to phantom losses that allow an investor to offset income for calculating income taxes.

Equity: the value of the owned portion of an asset. Equity is usually calculated as market value minus debt. In this book, equity is the portion of a real estate exchange that is in complete control of the seller and/or buyer for the assets they are exchanging.

Ethereum: the second most popular cryptocurrency. Ethereum was the genesis of smart contracts and digital applications.

Fiat currency: money issued by nations (for example, dollars, euros) is called fiat currency. The currency has value because the nations says it does (fiat). The term is usually used to distinguish from cryptocurrency.

Fungible/Non-fungible: a cryptocurrency is fungible if any two tokens are identical. Bitcoin and TROPTIONS are fungible. Smart contracts generally are not (they are unique tokens that represent a specific transaction). In regular currency, dollars are fungible. But a 1933 Saint-Gaudens Double Eagle (of which there are only a few in existence) is non-fungible. Any two may have different values based on their condition. Fungibility is important for exchange and trading.

Leasehold: a type of control of a property where the property is rented from the owner for a limited period of time.

Liquidity: the ability to sell a cryptocurrency for fiat. Today, most cryptocurrencies are non-liquid or minimally liquid (they can only be sold in small amounts).

Option: a type of control where the buyer prevents others from buying the property while assessing the viability of the property for purchase without owning the property. Usually an agreed purchase price is part of an option.

REXNET: Real Estate eXchange NETwork. A type of barter currency that uses proof of use as its valuation approach. The network includes a number of sub-tokens (for example, REXNET. Panama) that can be traded for each other as well as for assets.

Tokens vs coins: a coin is a cryptocurrency that has its own blockchain. A token is a cryptocurrency that is recorded on another coin's blockchain.

Trading pairs: trading pairs are the available exchanges on an exchange. For example, some tokens may only be traded for a handful of specific other tokens. To sell for cash, you often must trade your token for another; perhaps trade that one for Bitcoin and sell Bitcoin for cash. Trading pairs also impact valuation. If your trades are for Ripple and later Ripple goes down in value, it will appear that your coin also goes down in value unless new trades have happened that show your exchange rate with Ripple changing. This fact is important because it reduces the confidence you should have in the crypto values listed at popular exchange sites. When the values can change without new trades providing information, it calls into question the values listed.

TROPTIONS/XTROPTIONS.GOLD/XTROPTIONS/ XTROPTIONS. AUS/TROPTIONS.GOLD: the original barter cryptocurrencies. TROPTIONS were created (not on the blockchain) in 2003 as a way to trade options (Trade plus Options = TROPTIONS). In 2017 they were moved to the blockchain to obtain the benefits of immutability and easy trades. TROPTIONS have been used, perhaps more than any other cryptocurrency, for real estate transactions.

Value: the value of a cryptocurrency is how much it is worth, usually measured in dollars or Bitcoin. For cryptocurrencies, valuation can be very challenging. The most common way to value a cryptocurrency is to look at its most recent trades at an exchange. However, this is challenging, as the recent trades might be at different values. Further, some cryptocurrencies (for example, barter currencies) don't generally have both ends of the transaction (and thus the value) available on the block-chain. Value may also be defined more generally as the price at which a willing buyer and seller would trade an asset.

Wallet: a wallet is where cryptocurrency is stored. There are many different types for different uses, and often the type of crypto-currency will determine which wallets are feasible.

INTRODUCTION

Why a Book about Cryptocurrency AND Real Estate?

Cryptocurrency and one of its main underlying technologies, Block-chain, are poised to transform many industries. The currency aspect of cryptocurrency has potential to impact the whole idea of money, and the concept of a blockchain—when combined with other practices that make the data in the blockchain transparent and immutable—can impact any industry that keeps records.

Real estate, which tends to be a conservative, slow-to-change industry, is ripe for transformation by these technologies. Of course, real estate involves money, but real estate also has numerous areas where important and valuable records must be kept. Title records, leases, and contracts are important documents that need to remain dependably accurate in the long-term. Blockchain provides a trans-parent way of reliably recording and maintaining these transactions.

You might say that the combination of cryptocurrency and real estate are the Reese's Cup of investing. They are great apart, but when combined—WOW! Real estate is the chunky peanut butter, stable and filling. It's the type of asset most wealthy people use to maintain and grow their wealth. Cryptocurrency is the smooth chocolate, adding rapid appreciation and jumpstarting businesses. The combination provides wealth acceleration with safety for an incredibly satisfying investment approach.

How can real estate investors take advantage of Bitcoin and blockchain to set themselves apart from the crowd and improve their investing strategies and techniques?

That is the central question in this book. In it I explore several aspects of cryptocurrency and blockchain technology and how they relate to and impact real estate.

This book is for any real estate investor who may want to use the advantages of cryptocurrency in their investing. It is also for any cryptocurrency investor who might want to diversify into real estate or understand how to use cryptocurrency in new ways.

Cryptocurrency can act like cash—but without the devaluation inherent in government-issued money—and can be an attractive approach for sellers who want to exchange their equity for an appreciating asset instead of depreciating cash.

Cryptocurrency can also act like an asset, providing some interesting possibilities for property exchange and debt collateralization. It may be that cryptocurrency can mitigate tax consequences of sales as well. Cryptocurrency will transform buying and selling real estate.

There are several types of cryptocurrency. Bitcoin and barter currencies are like money. Other kinds of cryptocurrency can act as structures for real estate ownership (security token offerings) or can store real estate records such as title, leases, or liens (smart contracts) in an automated and immutable fashion. Still other types of cryptocurrency can implement loyalty programs for tenants in a cool and effective way. These types of cryptocurrencies will transform real estate ownership and transform real estate management.

All these transformations are at their very beginning stages. Astute real estate investors who learn how to take advantage of even a few of these opportunities will provide themselves with a competitive advantage over the next few years and will be poised to create wealth from the synergies between real estate and crypto-currency.

There are also huge opportunities for cryptocurrency investors who learn how to leverage their expertise with cryptocurrency to invest in real estate. Today, the vast majority of cryptocurrency investors act like speculators, trying to guess which cryptocurrencies will rise in value and when. They 'buy the dips' and look at candle charts, but they might as well be playing roulette. Many of these real estate related opportunities in cryptocurrency are true investment vehicles that rely on physical assets supporting the cryptocurrency and have regular cash flow. Others are solid business opportunities, where the cryptocurrency is really a modern (and better) approach to an age-old need. Investing in the types of approaches I describe in this book can reduce the volatility of cryptocurrency investing for cryptocurrency investors while accelerating wealth creation for real estate investors. We can get the best of both worlds.

I wrote this book because there are so many synergies between real estate and cryptocurrency, but most of both disciplines are fragmented. Even those who are at the forefront of combining real estate and cryptocurrency seem to be narrowly focused on one link. Some groups are working solely on smart contracts for real estate. Others are only doing tokenization. Still others look only at the buying and selling and finding new ways to structure real estate investment deals using cryptocurrency. I wanted to tie all these approaches together into a more comprehensive plan that will give us even greater linkages and synergies.

About the Author

Why me? Who am I to write this book? My background is unique. I started my career more years ago than I care to remember, working in cryptography. Since then, I have made a career of algorithm development and data analysis. I have developed sophisticated risk assessment methodologies. I have worked to apply artificial intelligence (AI) to stock and bond selection.

I started investing in real estate (beyond owning my own home) in 2004 after reading *Rich Dad, Poor Dad* by Robert Kiyosaki. I have been involved in a wide variety of investments, including single family homes, apartments, self-storage, mobile home parks, retail, development projects, and assisted living homes. And I am a member of one of the most creative deal-making groups in the country, the National Council of Exchangors (NCE). I have learned—and continue to learn—so much from these experts. My involvement has opened my eyes to many alternative ways to structure real estate deals. And it has shown me how to apply my algorithm development expertise to real estate investing.

In 2017, I was given an opportunity to trade land for cryptocurrency. I had heard of Bitcoin but had no idea of the whole new world of blockchain and crypto assets. As I did my due diligence, I got really excited about the combination. I did the deal (one of the largest direct exchanges of real estate for cryptocurrency ever done) and since then have continued to look for synergies between real estate and crypto. This book is a result of my unique journey and experience.

About this Book

The book is organized into four sections. This first section provides an introduction to both cryptocurrency and real estate investing. This is provided for those who know little to nothing about one or the other domain. But this section also ensures we are on the same page with regard to terminology that will be used throughout the book. Especially with real estate investing, I want to put a different spin on how we look at structuring real estate investments. A more general approach to understanding how real estate works will serve you well as I begin describing ways of structuring deals that include cryptocurrency. The principles are taken from a branch of real estate investing called real estate exchange. If you have done very traditional deals before (cash down payment, bank loan for the rest) this approach may be eye-opening in itself and could take your real estate investing to another level.

The second section considers how cryptocurrency will transform real estate deal-making. It covers various deal structures and how cryptocurrencies that act like currency work. I introduce a particular type of barter cryptocurrency that has shown itself to be a strong player in real estate purchases. I also talk about the mechanics of closing a deal that involves cryptocurrency (there are some quirks that must be handled).

The third section discusses how cryptocurrency will transform real estate ownership. The centerpiece of this discussion is security token offerings (STOs) that allow you to tokenize properties and revolutionize how real estate syndications are structured, with advantages for all involved. But I also discuss some real nuts and bolts ways that cryptocurrency will affect real estate ownership by storing important records like title and leases on a blockchain. There are pilot programs going on right now to put real estate title on the blockchain, and there are nascent efforts to put all types of property information into available, secure, and immutable forms. These could radically change how title searches and title insurance are done.

In the final section, section four, I discuss how cryptocurrency will transform real estate management and how cryptocurrency can provide efficiencies and competitive advantages for real estate investors who have tenants or customers. In a competitive world, techniques that set you apart from your competitors can be immensely valuable. Even such simple techniques as accepting cryptocurrency for rent payments could make a difference, especially in real estate segments such as student housing.

Finally, I summarize the strategies presented in each section with action plans (one plan for real estate investors and one for cryptocurrency investors) that will support your efforts to implement what I have outlined in this book. Knowledge is worth little unless it is used. Or, as my favorite podcast, *Real Estate Guys Radio*, likes to phrase it, 'Education for Effective Action.' That is what I hope you will take from this book.

The world of cryptocurrency and real estate is rapidly changing. New capabilities and opportunities emerge every month, if not every week. To stay up-to-date on the synergies of real estate and cryptocurrency can be very challenging. To make it easier to stay on top of industry changes, I have created a monthly newsletter on topics related to cryptocurrency and real estate, focusing on the intersection between them. I also provide updates in-between newsletters as new providers emerge or activity happens. I further curate relevant third-party sites and content to guide you through the maze of claims and information (and misinformation) to better inform your investment decisions.

I also have some availability to consult personally on projects at the nexus of real estate and cryptocurrency. My time is limited, and I am very selective about projects or opportunities I take on. But if you have a project, I may be able to help you buy or sell real estate with cryptocurrency. I can provide advice and suggestions for deal structuring. I can assist with your real estate related crypto project. I may even be a buyer for your real estate if it meets my criteria. You won't know if you don't ask. Contact me with your ideas. You can sign up for the newsletter or ask me about a project through https://CryptoREBook.com.

SECTION I

CHAPTER ONE

WHAT IS CRYPTOCURRENCY?

C RYPTOCURRENCY IS DIFFERENT TODAY than it was just a few years ago. As Bitcoin was rising in popularity, there was a flurry of innovation and excitement around the ideas and the technology of cryptocurrency. Now, rather than a few cryptocurrencies orbiting around Bitcoin and Ethereum, there are over 7,000 cryptocurrencies. Most of those are (or will be) dead ends, just as most of the dot com companies started in the late 90s went bankrupt. That innovation continues, however; it may be that the whole ecosystem of cryptocurrencies will be dramatically different in a few years.

In this chapter I give a brief history of money to set the context for cryptocurrency. I provide an overview of what cryptocurrency is, the different types of cryptocurrencies, and how they might be useful to real estate investors. In later chapters I dive deeper into each of these strategies and how they are implemented and used. All of these strategies are cutting edge. To date, they have been used only a few times. But the concept has been proven and the potential is there to make cryptocurrency a staple of real estate investing.

There will come a time when everyone uses these techniques just as everyone now markets real estate online.

A Brief History of Money

What is money? Money is usually defined as something that serves as a medium of exchange, a store of value, and a unit of account. How these qualities are embodied has changed enormously over time.

The history of money is strangely fascinating. From barter to gold coins to paper currency to electronic entries on a credit card or bank statement, money has evolved to be what it is today. At each stage there was an advantage to the trader, and in later stages, advantages to others emerged as well. Each stage came with increased risk and some disadvantages as well. Collectively, however, we have made these tradeoffs.

And yet, all the older forms of money are still around. Barter arrangements still exist (off the books). There are still gold and silver coins. Paper currency is still printed and issued by countries, though nowhere near the amounts of fiat currencies that exist.

Cryptocurrency is a small but significant next step in the evolution of money. And just like each step before it, it provides advantages and disadvantages as well as new risks. To understand the advantages better, it helps to discuss the previous steps and what we gained and lost.

When society transitioned from bartering to money, we got something that could more easily be transported and could be traded for any goods, not just one person's assets for another's. What we lost was some amount of intrinsic value. You can't eat gold or build with it. While it is desired, it is not necessary for life.

With the transition to demand notes, we improved on the transportability of the currency. Gold can be very heavy to carry, especially in large amounts. We lost even more in intrinsic value. Bank notes of any kind rely on the credibility of the issuer. As more notes became issued by countries, the credibility increased. For many years, no one questioned the full faith and guarantee of the United States, for example. But these notes were backed by gold. At least theoretically, one could trade in dollars, or marks, or lira, for their equivalent value in gold.

Then the U.S. went off the gold standard in 1971. Now currencies issued by countries are essentially new debt, not backed by anything tangible. Countries play games with their currency, intentionally devaluing the currency by ensuring that inflation is 'managed' at about 2 to 3% per year. The advantages gained here are primarily by countries and banks who now create new money with the stroke of a keyboard. The countries can then pay off their debt with dollars that have less purchasing power than the ones they originally borrowed—devaluing themselves out of debt. The requirement for paper representations of the currency has gradually declined, and many people lead largely electronic monetary lives. They are paid by electronic transfer and pay their bills with credit cards or e-checks or apps. Risks from computer failure or hacking, or from the government's ability to freeze electronic assets are hugely increased.

Modern currencies like dollars and euros are called into existence by creating debt and by the affirmation of federal reserves and banks that the currency is worth something. They are called **fiat currencies,** since they exist because the governments say so.

Into this environment steps cryptocurrency. Cryptocurrencies do not generally require faith or guarantee. They cannot be frozen by governments (if they follow the Bitcoin model) and in fact cannot really be controlled by governments. They have all the transportability of fiat currency (even more, since national boundaries cannot restrict their movement). And they don't automatically devalue. In these early days of cryptocurrency, there is a lot of volatility in value, but several approaches are being developed that may stabilize those values.

Cryptocurrency Overview

A **cryptocurrency** (or **crypto currency**) is a digital asset designed to work as a medium of exchange that uses cryptography to secure its transactions, to control the creation of additional units, and to verify the transfer of assets (https://en.wikipedia.org/wiki/Cryptocurrency). I will also use a shortcut term '**crypto**' in the book to refer to cryptocurrencies.

Bitcoin, which was created in 2009, was the first decentralized cryptocurrency. The decentralization is critical. Every wallet that holds Bitcoin and every exchange ever done with Bitcoin is stored in a distributed ledger called a **blockchain.** The ledgers are maintained by independent parties. Anyone can host a copy of the ledger on their own computers. About every 10 seconds, a new set of entries (called a block) is added to the ledger. This block is the latest in a chain of blocks that goes back through time and captures all the entries and transactions (thus, the term blockchain). There is a mechanism in place that allows each new block to be validated in conjunction with all the previous blocks. Without going into detail, it is this validation mechanism combined with the nature of the blockchain itself, combined with the public and distributed attributes that give users of cryptocurrencies confidence that the blockchain is accurate and immutable. It is also this combination of factors that made Bitcoin unique from all previous attempts at creating a digital currency (there were several). It is not necessary to trust the Bitcoin founders in order to trust the Bitcoin currency. To the extent that other cryptocurrencies follow this formula, they can also be trusted—at least with regard to the validity and immutability of transactions.

The terms **coin** and **token** are used to refer to cryptocurrencies. Technically, a coin is a cryptocurrency with its own blockchain. A token is a cryptocurrency recorded on the blockchain of another coin.

Cryptocurrencies really came into the public consciousness in 2017 when numerous groups issued initial coin offerings (ICO) and several of them raised hundreds of millions of dollars in investment. Speculation ran wild, and Bitcoin reached nearly $20,000 per coin. The amount of money raised caught the interest of regulators, and both the IRS (Internal Revenue Service) and the SEC (Securities and Exchange Commission) issued opinions about tax treatment of cryptocurrencies and whether they were securities under U.S. securities law. In 2017, just about anything with blockchain in its name appeared to be investable. Numerous approaches to cryptocurrency were launched. The speculation market has calmed considerably, and in its place is a more considered treatment of cryptocurrency that recognizes that, in fact, there are different types of tokens that have varying regulatory treatment and are useful for different purposes.

These multiple approaches or concepts for cryptocurrency come about because all of it is so new and the barriers to creating a cryptocurrency are so low that many people are able to try out their ideas. That is a critical factor in understanding cryptocurrency. While Bitcoin is the granddaddy of the current coins and tokens, there is a raft of creativity going into designing new tokens. The fact is that currencies represent something. Dollars represented gold and now represent debt. Bitcoin represents a value based on supply and demand. Other cryptocurrencies represent ownership in something: art, real estate, companies, debt. Some represent utility within an ecosystem. Still others represent an agreement between parties. Cryptocurrency as a whole is an electronic method for representing any of these things. Individual cryptocurrencies represent something more specific.

There are many terms and jargon associated with cryptocurrency. I will define the ones we need as we get to them. You can also refer to the compendium of useful terms in the front of this book as needed. I have used plain language definitions rather than technical ones and tied them to the book's theme of cryptocurrency and real estate when appropriate.

Types of Cryptocurrency

Cryptocurrencies are electronic tokens that can be created, stored, and traded. However, as cryptocurrencies have developed over the past few years, especially since 2017, several distinct types have evolved. Different authorities classify them differently, but for purposes of this book, I will talk about four types of cryptocurrencies:

Currencies: these are intended to act as digital money. They include Bitcoin and Litecoin and also include barter currencies like TROPTIONS (trade options) tokens and REXNET (real estate exchange network). Currencies are intended to act like digital money and are used to buy things. The IRS (usually) treats these cryptocurrencies as assets, and the SEC (usually) agrees that they are not securities. Currencies derive their value from the markets that accept them for payment. In this way, these currencies are just like dollars, euros, and other national currencies (fiat currencies). The value of a dollar is what you can buy with it, just as the value of a Bitcoin is what you can buy with it.

Security Tokens (STOs): there are many different security tokens, and these types of tokens, along with utility tokens, are likely to represent the greatest growth in the number of new tokens issued. Security tokens derive their value from ownership of an underlying asset, like a company (acting like stock in a company), real estate (representing ownership of a property or the LLC that owns it), or artwork (own a piece of a Picasso). These tokens are treated as securities by the SEC, so all securities laws must be followed when issuing, selling, or trading these tokens.

Utility Tokens: utility tokens represent value within a particular company for its products or services. Examples include game companies that issue tokens that can be redeemed within a game for additional characters or capabilities. One of the best examples of a utility token (though not a cryptocurrency, since it is not on a blockchain) is frequent flyer miles. Each mile is a digital token that is issued to airline customers when they buy tickets and can be redeemed with that airline for seat upgrades, free flights, etc. It would not be at all surprising for airlines to convert their frequent flyer programs to utility tokens; it would be a good fit and may have marketing advantages. There are a number of potential uses for utility tokens within real estate investing. These tokens may or may not be considered securities by the SEC, depending on the specific intent and use of the tokens.

Smart Contracts: though other types of tokens and coins may be issued as smart contracts, I call attention to this category because it has broad implications in real estate. Smart contracts can implement numerous contract capabilities in an agreed upon and automated way. Since the entire process of purchasing, selling, or investing in real estate involves contracts, new, faster, automated methods for implementing the transaction can be done via smart contracts.

Blockchain

All cryptocurrencies rely on the blockchain. At its simplest level, a blockchain is a distributed ledger that records exchanges. The ledger is distributed in that many people may keep independent copies of it that are verified against each other. At regular intervals, a new block containing transactions is added in sequence to form a chain of blocks (or blockchain). All of the old blocks are preserved and their validity ensured using a cryptographic algorithm called a hash code. There are many books that go into detail of how a blockchain works, but for purposes of this book, it is important to know what the advantages are to having a blockchain.

When a blockchain is publicly maintained by independent parties (like with Bitcoin and Ethereum), there are many copies of the chain, all of which are secured by cryptography. Each added block involves solving a challenging cryptographic algorithm that requires substantial computing power. To change a previous block requires solving that problem again, not only for that block but for all blocks that ensue. The work involved makes changing a block extremely difficult and also requires collusion of 51% or more of the people who are maintaining the blocks. These challenges combined make the public blockchains 'immutable'. Every transaction can be relied upon to be what was recorded. This feature makes storage on the blockchain extremely secure.

As cryptocurrencies proliferate, however, many newer coins create their own private blockchain, and many financial organizations also create private blockchains to store their transactions. They rely on the reputation of Bitcoin to be immutable, but a private blockchain does not have that property. Since one owner owns all the copies of a private blockchain, they can go back and change all the copies at once, potentially modifying transactions that happened in the past. It is only the fact that blockchains are public, maintained by numerous independent parties, and that someone wanting to change the blockchain would have to redo all the work of creating blocks after the changed block that makes a blockchain immutable.

Different blockchains have different intervals for when a new block is created (Bitcoin is 10 seconds). They also have different sizes of blocks and different information that must be recorded. These factors impact the speed at which transactions may be completed. Bitcoin, for example, has had issues when transaction volume has increased. Sometimes it may take hours or even days for a transaction to be written to the blockchain. Some of these issues have been addressed with changes to the content of the blocks and with increased block size, but they could remain issues if the number of transactions continues to increase.

For some of the more complicated tokens like STOs and smart contracts, an approach to maintaining transaction immutability and speed without cluttering up the public blockchain with detailed contract information is to store the transaction itself on a blockchain and the detailed information elsewhere, on a **sidechain**. The sidechain may be maintained privately because the immutability of the transaction itself is assured by the public blockchain. This approach is becoming universal for the creation of STOs that must maintain SEC rules for buying and selling the tokens within its smart contract.

Now that I have introduced the different types of crypto to give a broad understanding of their differences, I will go into more detail on each type.

Currency Tokens

The best-known cryptocurrency is Bitcoin. Bitcoin was the original coin that used the blockchain and all the other strategies to ensure a reliable, transparent, immutable coin. Bitcoin, like all currency coins or tokens, gains its value from being accepted in trades and for goods and services. Currently (2021) Bitcoin is accepted at over 70,000 retailers, and the daily market is strong enough that Bitcoin may be bought or sold readily and in fairly large amounts (millions of dollars' worth). Both Bitcoin and Bitcoin Cash (BTC) are extremely liquid. Several other currency coins are also quite liquid though at lower amounts than Bitcoin. Litecoin is an example of those.

Currency tokens are not treated as securities (in the U.S.). They are typically characterized as assets. From an IRS standpoint, it is important to calculate your basis in the coin when you acquire it and compare that to your price when you sell it. You may be responsible for capital gains or be able to deduct capital losses when you sell. If you exchange for another asset, there are differing opinions about what must be declared or paid. You should discuss this with your accountant; it is likely that these rapidly changing rules will be clarified or updated. For example, the 2020 tax forms require taxpayers to check a box indicating whether they have acquired or sold cryptocurrency during the year. This is widely understood to indicate that the IRS will increase auditing and enforcement of capital gains taxes from sales of cryptocurrency.

Since currency tokens are intended to be treated as digital money, their benefit (and usually their value) depends largely on the size of the market where they can be used as digital money. In the early days of Bitcoin, there was little to no market in the real world for the coins. In fact, in 2010, Laszlo Hanyecz bought two Papa John's pizzas for 10,000 BTC (BTC is the symbol for Bitcoin). This was one of the first transactions for a real-world item. At the end of 2017, when Bitcoin was selling for nearly $20,000, those two pizzas cost $200M. Though one must wonder if Bitcoin would ever have gotten to that price without those early transactions.

The key for currency tokens then is where you can use them. In 2020, there are numerous places to use Bitcoin, but very few to use other cryptocurrencies. The vast majority of currency tokens can only be traded for other currency tokens on a cryptocurrency exchange. Will they become as liquid as Bitcoin? The answer for most of them is likely no. But currency tokens that become liquid will almost certainly also increase in value.

Within the broad category of currency tokens there are a couple of subcategories that are worth mentioning. The first of these are stable coins. Stable coins are designed to reduce volatility by pegging their value to something else. The first stable coins pegged their value to gold, essentially creating currencies on the gold standard. But most of the more popular stable coins peg their values to fiat currencies like the U.S. dollar. Tether, the most popular stable coin, holds dollars in reserve in order to make its price always equal to $1. I really don't understand why tying value to a consistently depreciating asset deserves the label 'stable'. But that is what is happening. I won't be discussing stable coins in this book but want to mention them here for the sake of completeness.

The other subcategory I will discuss extensively in this book is barter currency. Barter currency is distinguished by its emphasis on direct exchange for goods and services rather than being exchanged on crypto exchanges. These currencies, particularly TROPTIONS tokens and REXNET, may be the best tokens for use in real estate deals.

Utility Tokens

Utility tokens are used to pay for goods or services within a company. There are many potential uses for this type of cryptocurrency. One key use that is important to real estate is to implement loyalty programs. Another is to create an internal currency within a company that can be used as an alternative to cash. Before the creation of cryptocurrencies there were, and are, numerous other approaches to internal utility. When you go to a casino, you trade your fiat currency for chips that are only good as money within the casino. When you book a flight, you may be issued miles that can be redeemed for new flights or seat upgrades—but only with that airline or its affiliates. Years ago, you could get green stamps at a cash register that you could paste in a book and later redeem for goods.

Utility tokens are just a new way of issuing, tracking, and exchanging those same sorts of things. But they come with advantages in that they could be traded on an exchange, could have liquidity, or could be exchanged for other utility tokens, and can be easily accessed from anywhere since they are electronic. Issuing these tokens on a blockchain provides these advantages.

The most popular utility token by far is Ethereum. Ethereum and its token, Ether, were created to provide a framework for smart contracts. Ether is used as 'gas' to fuel the recording of smart contracts on its blockchain. But there are numerous other tokens. One that became extremely popular in 2017 was Cryptokitties. Cryptokitties was a game where you could collect and breed digital cats. You pay for game features and capabilities using its internal utility token. As we will see, there are several ways to use utility tokens in a real estate business.

Security Tokens

Security Token Offerings (STOs) use cryptocurrency to represent ownership of some underlying asset. The first such tokens were created to represent ownership in the companies issuing the tokens. Many of these companies were created in 2017 and launched their token sales as initial coin offerings (ICOs) in direct mimicry of initial public offerings (IPOs). The usual formula was for the company to create a 'white paper' describing the new and innovative capability that the company intended to develop. They issued their coins or tokens as a way of raising money for the company to actually develop what they promised.

Of course, IPOs are heavily regulated by the Securities and Exchange Commission (SEC) in the U.S. and by other securities organizations in other countries. But many companies thought they could get away with ICOs since they were not yet directly regulated. Many of those companies found out differently.

In the U.S., whether an issuance of any kind is considered to be a security is controlled by the 'Howey Test', named after the legal case in which the test was first described. A security is 1) an investment of money 2) in a common enterprise 3) with the expectation of profit 4) derived solely from the efforts of a third party. It was really clear that any ICO that involved investing in a company and expecting to derive profit from the activities of the company would be a security.

While the initial security tokens were primarily investments in companies—essentially a modern method of issuing stock—as crypto has evolved, STOs have been issued to tokenize other types of assets (notably real estate). Various platforms have been created to issue security tokens, many of them explicitly and automatically enforcing the SEC purchase and sale regulations and working within the existing private placement offering regulations like Regulation D, Regulation A, and Regulation S.

STOs are still in their infancy. Most of the companies that assist with issuing STOs do not yet do business in the U.S. because of its more stringent securities regulations. The number of actual STOs (not accidental STOs created during the ICO boom) is in the tens right now, and the number of real estate STOs can be counted on one's fingers. But the framework and proof of concept has been created, and the industry is poised to explode with new STOs, both for companies and for tokenizing real estate.

Smart Contracts

Smart contracts are unusual in the cryptocurrency world. Most digital assets are fungible. One Bitcoin is exactly identical in function and form (and value) to any other Bitcoin. One TROPTION is identical to any other TROPTION. Those coins and tokens are fungible. Smart contracts are not. One smart contract might be a real estate purchase between me and a seller; another might be a title issued by a seller to a buyer. These tokens are not interchangeable, so they are not fungible.

While smart contracts might be recorded on a public blockchain so that the fact of the contract is immutable and public, the actual details of the smart contract can be kept private among the parties.

Smart contracts were initially enabled by the Ethereum blockchain and its underlying code. The code allowed digital applications (DAPPs) to be created that could implement any sort of contract. The contracts could be automatically executed when the conditions within them were met. This approach was a huge change (many would say advance) over the original Bitcoin blockchain approach that only supported documenting transactions.

Most companies that support smart contracts create a utility token that acts as a processing fee or recording fee for the actual smart contract. You pay the fee in their utility token and they ensure that the smart contract is recorded on the blockchain.

Why Cryptocurrency?

There have been many attempts to create digital currencies over the years, all of which failed prior to the advent of Bitcoin. Rather than belabor what went wrong, let's talk about what Bitcoin got right. Bitcoin is on a public blockchain that is secured by cryptography that prevents modification of the blockchain by someone wishing to subvert the currency. Bitcoin rewards those who help maintain the transaction blockchain (so-called miners) by issuing new Bitcoin each time the blockchain is updated. The number of Bitcoin issued halves at specified intervals, which means that there will never be more than 21,000,000 Bitcoin issued. This type of asymptotic issuance ensures scarcity in Bitcoin. No one can just create more Bitcoin like countries create fiat.

Bitcoin is supported by public volunteers. The Bitcoin software is also open source so that anyone can view, understand, and debug it. This openness provides confidence in the source and prevents government authorities from controlling Bitcoin issuance, storage, or trades. Bitcoin accomplishes this peer-to-peer coordination by solving something known as the Byzantine Generals Problem (essentially consensus generation in the absence of a secure communication).

Bitcoin can be subdivided up to 10^{-8}. Fiat currencies usually have only two decimal points of division (think about the penny being one 100th of a dollar). This helps alleviate the scarcity of Bitcoin (there will never be more than 21 million of them) by allowing the price of Bitcoin to rise so that fractions of Bitcoin can become the standard trades. In mid-2020 you could buy .001 Bitcoin for about $10, but you could sell as little as .00000001 Bitcoin, which would cost one 1000th of a penny. That smallest amount of Bitcoin is called a Satoshi after Bitcoin's legendary creator.

The biggest impact of subdivision is improved liquidity. The market for something that costs $10,000 is much smaller than the market for something that costs $10.

The openness of Bitcoin also results in two extremely desirable properties for those who would like to see currencies free from manipulation. First, Bitcoin cannot be stopped, seized, or frozen by governments. Since governments have shown an inability to be responsible with money (moving away from the gold standard, printing money to ensure that the money depreciates in value each year, manipulating their currency's value against others), removing a currency from government control may have long-term advantages. The inability of governments to control the currency also means that Bitcoin is borderless and can be exchanged anywhere without the possibility of intervention.

In addition, the openness of Bitcoin and the structure of its blockchain, mining, and issuance approach ensures the immutability of Bitcoin transactions. Coins cannot be double spent. Any trade will immediately be publicly known and cannot be reversed. And any wallet address holding Bitcoin is perpetually credited with the coins. This is a necessary (but not sufficient) condition for a currency to be a store of value.

But Bitcoin is only one attempt at digital currency. Building on the solutions for consensus that Bitcoin implemented, other cryptocurrencies have made modifications to accomplish other goals (enhanced privacy, faster transaction times, cheaper transactions, etc.). One cryptocurrency, Ethereum, however, has made a substantial adaptation to what is stored on the Blockchain. Ethereum introduced 'smart contracts' that can be recorded and modified on a blockchain, essentially making the contracts themselves immutable. Ethereum's crypto is called Ether. Ether is mainly a utility token because it allows you to record smart contracts or even digital applications (called DAPPs) on the Ethereum blockchain. Colloquially referred to as the 'gas' that fuels the DAPPs, Ether is the second most traded (and highest capitalized) crypto. The concept of smart contracts will be extremely important for many real estate applications and is described in later chapters.

I should also mention another type of cryptocurrency you won't read about in most crypto articles or hear about in even the most technical crypto discussions. This is a type of currency focused on being used in transactions. These cryptocurrencies are an outgrowth of barter currencies. In the history of money, the very first type of trade was barter. That was largely replaced by gold and later paper currency. But there have always been alternative currencies accepted by groups of people (think of poker chips at a casino or International Trade Exchange—ITEX). A few forward-thinking people have created barter currencies on a blockchain. These currencies act something like Bitcoin, and they are a subclass within the currency type of coin, but where Bitcoin is usually used to trade for fiat, these currencies are usually used to trade directly for assets (like real estate). These cryptocurrencies are especially relevant for real estate deal-making.

Evaluating Cryptocurrency for Investment

What does it actually mean to invest in a cryptocurrency? And what criteria should an investor look for in a cryptocurrency?

Investments in cryptocurrency can be understood by comparing them to other kinds of investments. The investments that people understand the best may be stocks. Stocks are partial ownership of a company. When an investor invests in stocks, most of the time they are really looking for the price to go up—appreciation. Alternatively, an investor might be looking for dividends paid by the stocks. Dividends are cash flow. But most stock investors are looking for appreciation. How do they know whether a stock is going to go up or not? That can be very much like a roller coaster and is the subject of numerous books, software programs, and schemes.

Whether a stock appreciates has a lot to do with both the company's fundamentals—how well the company does its business, whether it's growing, whether its bottom line is increasing—and also how the market perceives the company and how investors perceive the market.

Market perceptions encompass a whole set of factors about the momentum of the stock and the momentum of the market and where everything's going, and those perceptions influence the price of a stock.

Bonds—debt owed by a company or government—have similar characteristics. With bonds, you worry about the fundamentals of the organization, which are reflected in its credit rating. Then you look at the interest rates and whether the interest rate on the bond will be attractive if market interest rates are changing. If interest rates go up, the bond will become less valuable. If interest rates go down, the bond might become more valuable.

When investors evaluate a cryptocurrency, however, there aren't the same kind of fundamentals that are present with a stock.

There are really three questions to ask about cryptocurrency when evaluating it for investment, and two of them are questions that are not always asked with stocks or bonds. The first question is, "What will the value of the cryptocurrency be?" You also ask this question with stocks and bonds.

The second question is, "Can I sell it?" Now that's something you don't ask as much with stocks or bonds. Generally, the market is large enough on the list of exchanges that if the stock is issued by a publicly traded company, you can sell it.

And similarly, with a bond, the bond markets, while more fragmented than the stock markets, are still quite large. If you have a bond from a company, the chances are pretty good that you can go to a bond broker and sell it.

This isn't always true of cryptocurrency. Being able to sell a cryptocurrency at any significant scale is a feature that applies only to a few cryptocurrencies. Being able to sell an investment, referred to as liquidity, is a serious issue for almost all cryptocurrencies.

Then the third question is, "Can I use the cryptocurrency in some other way than selling it?" Many cryptocurrencies have uses within a particular company ecosystem and can essentially be consumed. If you have need of the services that the cryptocurrency enables, investing in the cryptocurrency may be valuable to you even if you cannot sell it or it does not increase in value.

To summarize, the questions to ask when you want to invest are: Will the cryptocurrency go up in value? Can I use the cryptocurrency for something that benefits me? If the cryptocurrency increases in value, will I then be able to sell it and move into a different asset class?

The answer to those questions will be different for the different kinds of cryptocurrency.

There is one more piece of background that is necessary to understand about investing in cryptocurrencies. This applies mainly to cryptocurrencies that are used as currencies.

Is cryptocurrency money? Not everyone agrees. But cryptocurrency certainly seems to do much of what money does. It seems clear that cryptocurrency is a unit of account, since it is quantitative and priced. It is common for one cryptocurrency to be denominated in another (its trading pair). It's very clear that the token is a unit and a subdivided unit, and it's very easy to understand what that is.

Whether cryptocurrency is a store of value probably depends on whether we think that cryptocurrency can appreciate. If the value of the cryptocurrency can go to zero, if it goes away, or becomes unused, then it would certainly not be a store of value. But cryptocurrency that maintains or increases its value would act as a store of value. Some point to the price volatility of crypto as proving that crypto cannot be a store of value. But I disagree. Short-term fluctuations do not necessarily affect crypto as a store of value. It is more important to look at medium- to long-term trends instead. Certainly with Bitcoin, the trend over the past five years has been a substantial increase in value.

Is cryptocurrency a medium of exchange? Most cryptocurrencies aren't very popular as a medium of exchange. Virtually all cryptocurrencies are limited to crypto exchanges for their use. Today, Bitcoin is an exception. As of today, Bitcoin is accepted at over 70,000 retailers of various types. Ethereum is a distant second, but is gaining acceptance.

Bitcoin has also become more common in places where the national currency is in free fall such as Venezuela, Cyprus, and Greece. People are fleeing to Bitcoin there because it has become a very good medium of exchange. And it is a far better store of value than the local currency.

Most other cryptocurrencies are not usable as a medium of exchange, and it's hard to trade them for something else. I'll revisit this discussion when I present barter currencies that represent an alternative approach to becoming a medium of exchange.

Within the context of how to evaluate cryptocurrencies as an investment, I can now look at the different kinds of cryptocurrency, how they're influenced by liquidity and value, and how to how to look at them as an investment.

The first to consider, of course, are those cryptocurrencies that are currencies. Many crypto investors use analytic approaches that mimic how they evaluate stock selection. They talk about techniques like candle charts. They propose 'buying the dips' and looking at patterns of activity. There is even a discussion about whether the fundamentals are sound.

But, the language used, which is borrowed from the language of stocks and bonds, is not really accurate when applied to cryptocurrencies. There really aren't fundamentals in the same sense that there are for stocks.

Fundamentals, when evaluating stocks and bonds, are that the company actually provides goods and services. Those goods and services are in demand, and the company may be expected to provide more or less of them, increase prices, or be forced to decrease them.

For most cryptocurrencies, a discussion of the fundamentals is not valid, and there's no real reason to believe any of the other patterns that people discuss endlessly would apply to cryptocurrencies or that there even is a pattern to its ups and downs.

Frankly, there may not be patterns to stocks' ups and downs that can truly be captured as abstract patterns. It's more likely that stock movements are triggered by something that's actually going on in the world. But it is even more important to be careful when using those sorts of investment approaches to talk about cryptocurrency.

When it comes to cryptocurrencies that act as currencies, the biggest question is liquidity. If you're trying to use a cryptocurrency as a medium of exchange, you have to be able to exchange it for something else. But when a cryptocurrency is launched, it is not very good for a medium of exchange. It doesn't have much of a market, doesn't have many people invested in it, and there aren't many people who know about it. And so, it's very hard to sell it.

Almost all cryptocurrencies are only exchanged on crypto exchanges. And most cryptocurrencies only trade for other cryptocurrencies, known as their trading pairs. Very few cryptocurrencies act as portals to fiat currency. All the other cryptocurrencies must go through these few to obtain liquidity.

The top five or six cryptocurrencies (Bitcoin, Ether, Litecoin, etc.) can be traded directly for fiat. Almost all the other cryptocurrencies have to be traded through one of these top six or so to get to fiat, which really puts a crimp on them being a medium of exchange.

As a crypto becomes more popular and gets used more, this can change. The cryptocurrencies that are currently in vogue were certainly not media of exchange when they were first launched, and it took them a while to get to that point. For a new cryptocurrency that is being launched, one must ask if and when the cryptocurrency will become a medium of exchange.

Barter currencies are quite interesting in this respect because instead of being exchanged on a crypto exchange, they can be directly exchanged for assets. Barter provides an alternative way of exchanging the coins or tokens for something of value and potentially opens the tokens to new markets and people beyond those who participate in cryptocurrency exchanges.

Trading for assets is a form of liquidity; it does create and store value, but it is not an approach that is as common to cryptocurrencies. Most crypto asset holders don't understand the idea of bartering cryptocurrencies. It's a matter of putting a couple of different worlds together here and coming up with a new approach.

Moving beyond looking at cryptocurrencies that are designed to be money, I will deal with utility tokens next.

The biggest question an investor should ask about utility tokens is, "What value does it provide to a user?" One might invest in the utility token because one wishes to use the functions within that company site that the utility token pays for. That would be a perfectly valid reason to invest and has nothing to do with value or liquidity. The liquidity is sort of built-in because you use the services of the site.

There may also be investors who are not actually wanting to use the tokens within the site. They want to hold the tokens with the idea that they may go up in value and can later sell them to other people who would use the utility on the site. Investors with that objective will ask questions about the popularity of the site and how often people will be using it and how easy it is for them to buy from the investor instead of from the site itself.

The answers will be different for different tokens, but these really have little application to real estate except when it's a real estate company creating utility within its own ecosystem, which I will discuss in later chapters.

The third type of cryptocurrency is the security token. The security token does act very much like a stock because its value is the value of the underlying assets, as well as the credibility of the offerors and the risk. The underlying asset could be a company. In that case, the security token acts exactly like a stock share. The value of the company tells you what the price of the token ought to be. And if the company is going up in value, one would expect the security token to rise in value commensurately.

If the company pays dividends, the token holder usually receives those dividends in cash as opposed to cryptocurrency. A security token that represents a company is essentially a stock but tradable on a crypto exchange rather than a stock exchange.

A security token could also represent ownership of a piece of real estate or something else of value. Security tokens could be backed by gold, real estate, a Picasso, or something else. Again, the value of the token is the value of the underlying asset.

For real estate, a security token acts a lot like a private placement memorandum or private offering and, in fact, in the U.S., one would expect that the issuer would have to go through the same rules as a private offering in order to offer the tokens to the investors.

But for something like gold, gems, or a Picasso, the security token represents some new type of ownership. Now the issue arises of how likely you are to be able to receive your portion of the underlying asset value. If you have a Picasso, obviously you can't cut off a little piece of that and take it with you. It would destroy the value of the painting. You have to believe that the issuers are taking good care of the painting and that the painting is protected and insured. If the painting goes up in value and it's sold, the value would be distributed to the security token holders, and the security tokens would go away.

Tokenizing underlying assets like a piece of real estate, a Picasso, or gold are all potential uses for security tokens. An investor would want to know the value of the asset. An investor would also want to know whether the offerors are able to ensure that the value is retained or increased. They would evaluate the credibility of the issuers, just as an investor would evaluate the management of a company or the issuers of a private offering.

To summarize, a security token is evaluated in the same manner that an investor would evaluate other methods of owning similar assets like companies, real estate, art, or gold.

The last type of cryptocurrency to discuss is smart contracts. Remember that these are non-fungible tokens, and there is usually not an investment in a smart contract. Usually if you're investing, you invest in the utility token that provides access to the smart contracts. The contracts themselves are not so much investments but services.

Using Cryptocurrency in Real Estate

So how can these different types of cryptocurrency be used in real estate investing? There are numerous approaches. In this book I group them into three areas.

Transforming Deal-making

The primary investment approach is the purchase of real estate using cryptocurrency. This is one of the most obvious approaches. It uses currency tokens or coins and allows an investor to combine the rapid increase in value and some level of liquidity of the cryptocurrency with the stability, tax advantages, and leverage of real estate. To date, most of the purchases of real estate with cryptocurrencies have been two-stage transactions (sell the cryptocurrency for cash and use the cash to buy the real estate). But there have been some notable transactions of cryptocurrency directly exchanged for real estate. Cryptocurrency has especially strong potential for international sales, since it is so easy to move the currencies without respect to borders (it will be interesting to see how regulators end up addressing this). I devote Section II to discussing cryptocurrency in deal-making.

Transforming Ownership

The principal ownership transformation is in issuing security tokens as part of a real estate syndication. When purchasing large properties, it is often the case that a single buyer doesn't have the funds or the net worth to buy the property. One way to be able to purchase a large property is to pool funds and net worth from multiple investors. This is called a syndication, and it is often done in the U.S. by creating a private offering under Regulation D of the U.S. Securities and Exchange Commission (SEC) regulations. It's not necessary to understand all of that right now. I will explain in more detail in Section III. Traditional real estate syndications have several challenges, including managing investors' shares, handling the know-your-customer (KYC) and anti-money-laundering (AML) requirements, as well as privacy requirements in Europe. Most important is the illiquidity of private offerings. Security tokens can address all of these issues. They can make investor management much more automated and transparent and have the potential to increase liquidity, as long as the tokens are available on an exchange that enforces all the securities regulations using smart contracts.

Another way of transforming ownership is putting real estate title and other important documents on the blockchain. Nothing should be more immutable than real estate title. Having it recorded on a public blockchain that is readily searchable by anyone and that can include the necessary details (supported by smart contracts) can greatly simplify the search, management, and recording of title. At present only prototype efforts are underway, but this application of blockchain to real estate has the potential to speed transactions and reduce the cost of title searches and title insurance. In a similar way, putting sale listings on a searchable blockchain may also impact the current multiple listing services and provide a better capability for real estate investors. Another type of real estate contract called a ground lease may last for tens or even hundreds of years. Maintaining the ground lease information on a blockchain as a smart contract would make the management and monitoring of ground leases much easier.

Hosting real estate contracts on the blockchain is another game changer. Using smart contracts to implement letters of intent, contract offers, and all the legal stages of real estate can speed the negotiation time of an offer (since all parties can see the current state of the contract at all times) and actually execute important stages of the contract (such as distributing deposit funds) based on the contract terms. As the terms themselves become digitized, it will be easier to construct contracts from terms where the wording is more standardized, making for fewer contract disputes.

Transforming Management

In Section IV, I talk about using cryptocurrency in your real estate investment business. A key focus is developing loyalty or savings programs for rentals. Utility tokens have a number of uses in real estate investments. If tokens are issued to renters at an apartment complex, they can be saved up for a new amenity (like a ceiling fan or complimentary cleaning), used to defray rent, or used for a desired service like valet trash. The tokens would act as a loyalty program, providing renters with an advantage for staying at your property that could not easily be transferred to another property (just as the frequent flyer miles make you want to fly that airline to build up your miles).

Summary

Cryptocurrency is an important advance in the history of money. Crypto has numerous advantages over the current fiat currencies and is poised to take over many of the functions of fiat in the not-so-distant future. These advantages have huge implications for real estate investing. Even today it is possible to buy real estate with cryptocurrency, providing advantages to both the buyer and the seller. It is also possible to tokenize property ownership, making ownership available to the masses, just like large companies can be owned by anyone by buying stock. But cryptocurrency is so new that it is rapidly evolving. The cryptocurrency landscape today is far different than it was in 2017 when crypto beyond Bitcoin emerged. Cryptocurrency is evolving at the speed of the internet. Understanding the current basics and uses of cryptocurrency will allow an investor to keep up as new capabilities and features emerge.

CHAPTER TWO

REAL ESTATE INVESTING OVERVIEW

M ANY HAVE WRITTEN BOOKS on investing in real estate, and there are numerous valuable techniques and approaches in those books. I don't want to duplicate any of that here. Instead, what I want to do is to describe an approach to real estate investing and a way of looking at investments that is a little outside the usual approach. I also want to make sure that we are on the same page in terms of terminology (there are many different definitions of real estate terms that are either wrong or too narrow for our purposes). I hope you will bear with me, even if you already know real estate investing. I think characterizing investments the way I intend to here will make the later discussions about cryptocurrency combined with real estate easier to understand (and easier to communicate for me).

Any discussion of investments should start with the objectives of the investor. If you don't know what you are trying to accomplish by investing, it is hard to select investments that accomplish your goals. As the Cheshire Cat says to Alice in Lewis Carroll's *Alice in Wonderland,* "If you don't know where you are going, any road will get you there." Once you know your objectives, you can look at the types of return that help you accomplish them. And only then can you identify how to structure deals that will get you the returns that accomplish your objectives. That is the process we will follow in discussing real estate investing.

Investment Objectives

Every individual investor should examine their investment goals in detail. Typically, those goals are some combination of the following:

- **Income.** The investor is looking for the investments to provide a regular stream of money. For many investors this is the primary goal—to generate so-called 'passive' income. As Robert Kiyosaki outlines in his works, when your passive income exceeds your expenses, you are out of the rat race and you no longer need to hold a job or actively run a business. Getting out of the rat race is often a primary objective of real estate investors.

- **Wealth.** The investor is looking for the value of their assets to increase. The assets can then work in an upward spiral to continue to increase wealth. Wealth and income work in tandem; as wealth increases, income increases—provided the level of return stays the same.

- **Tax shelter.** Wealth is not just what you make from your investments but what you keep. Some investments may have the primary objective of reducing overall taxes so that more income/wealth can be retained.

- **Preservation.** Safety of investment is the inverse of risk of loss. Every investment has some risk of loss and some prospect of return. In stocks and bonds, the risk is almost always correlated with return. In real estate, which is not an efficient market, it is often possible to obtain large returns without increasing (and sometimes even reducing) risk. Each investor has levels of risk that they are willing to accept for particular investments. Sometimes that level is different for different parts of an investor's portfolio.

Every investor and every investment should be selected with the investor's goals in mind. In practice, most investors have some combination of the above goals and the goals themselves support each other in a synergistic way. Income beyond what is needed to pay the investor's expenses can be reinvested to increase wealth. Increased wealth can result in increased income. And reduced taxes can increase both wealth and income. As wealth increases, the level of acceptable risk often decreases for an investor. But for each investment, there is usually one particular objective that dominates, and different investment types better support different investment goals.

Investment Returns

An investor's objectives are mirrored in the types of return that can be obtained from a real estate investment. Real estate provides returns in essentially four ways:

- **Cashflow.** When real estate is rented, the rents provide income. A good investment will result in income that exceeds expenses that can then provide income to the investor. Cashflow is more specifically described as cash-on-cash return. It measures how much actual money is thrown off by the investment as a percentage of the total investment (cash/investment).
- **Principal.** Real estate is usually acquired using leverage (loans). The amount borrowed is called the principal. As the

loan is paid back (ideally by the rent from the tenants) the investor owes less on the property. The investor's ownership value (equity) increases as the loan is paid down. This process increases the investor's wealth.

- **Appreciation.** Historically, over time, real estate has increased in value. This increase in value is called appreciation. Appreciation comes in two types: market appreciation and forced appreciation. Market appreciation is the increase in value due to changes in market conditions. A house that was worth $250,000 five years ago may be worth $325,000 today. Forced appreciation comes from improving the property in some way. A vacant lot is more valuable once a house is built on it. Similarly, with commercial properties where the value is based on the income of the property, increasing the income through reduced vacancy, higher rents, property improvements, or reduced expenses can force the increase of the value through increase in income.

- **Tax advantages.** Real estate provides substantial tax advantages. The primary advantages are using depreciation to reduce income tax and using a tax deferred exchange (also called a 1031 exchange) to transition from one investment to another without paying capital gains taxes. But there are numerous tax credits and incentives for various real estate activities. In some cases, these advantages can offset income from other investments as well.

Perhaps the biggest advantage for investing in real estate is the use of leverage. While stocks and bonds are (usually) purchased 100% with cash, real estate is most commonly purchased with a loan for a substantial portion of the cost. When the loan interest rate is less than the income rate for the property, you are said to have positive leverage. The use of leverage can turbo charge your returns.

The following example shows the various returns you might receive. Suppose you purchase a property for $1,000,000 using an 80% loan ($800,000) at 5% interest, and the property throws off 9% of its value in income. The income from the property is $90,000 per year. The debt service on the loan (amortized over 25 years) will be $56,120 each year. Suppose that between reducing costs and increasing rents, the income for the property increases to $95,000 per year. And finally, suppose that the investor has a marginal income tax rate of 30% (including state and local) and that the property is depreciated in a straight line over 27 years.

Okay, that's a lot of numbers. I get it. Here are the anticipated returns given all that information. Don't worry about the mathematics behind it. This is not a book about mathematics. I just want to illustrate the types of returns and how leverage improves them.

- Cashflow = $33,880 (this is the cash-on-cash return).
- Principal reduction = $16,495 (how much principal was paid off during the first year).
- Forced appreciation = $55,555 (this is the increased value of the property due to the forced appreciation from increasing the income and keeping the capitalization rate constant at 9%). I am not assuming any market appreciation, but if the new market capitalization rate had dropped to 8.5%, there would be an additional $62,000 in appreciation from the market.
- Depreciation = $11,111 (this is the tax savings from depreciating the property – $37,037 tax deduction each year for 27 years at a 30% marginal tax rate).
- Total return for one year: $117,041 (the sum of all the other returns). This is a total return of 58.5%.

If I hadn't used leverage and had purchased the property all cash (similar to what we would get with a stock or bond that returned 9% and had no tax advantages), I would have a return of 9%. The advantages of real estate push that up to 58.5% and, really, could be even higher if other, more sophisticated techniques like cost segregation or market capital rate improvement come into play.

And yet, this is not a speculative investment type. These types of returns could come from an apartment complex or a self-storage facility. These returns could be achieved with an investment that is about as risky as purchasing stock in a utility company. Also note that because of the acceleration of principal payments that happens throughout the loan, the return of principal will increase every year.

Deal Structures

There is a very simple framework for how to structure real estate investments. As a real estate investor, you should view every investment though the lens of debt, equity, and control.

Debt refers to loans. Since most real estate is purchased with some amount of debt, that debt has to be accounted for in structuring a real estate deal. In essence, there is a party besides the owner who has an interest in the property that is usually secured by a lien. The amount of debt constrains the owner in what he can do in selling the property. Generally, debt must be paid off, assumed, refinanced, forgiven, or moved to another property. In the vast majority of real estate deals, the debt is paid off and new debt is placed against the property.

Equity is the difference between the value of the property and the amount of debt owed. It represents what the owner of the property actually owns. Because the owner owns the equity, she can do with it whatever she wants. She can accept a loan against it, give some or all of it away, trade it for another asset or a service, or accept a piece of real estate. In this book, of course, we will consider the option of accepting cryptocurrency for her equity. The important point here is that the owner has a lot of discretion on how to dispose of equity as part of a real estate deal. The only constraint might be her own objectives and the objectives of any partners in the real estate ownership.

The third component of structuring a real estate deal is **control.** This represents what interest a person has in a property. Most investors have fee simple ownership of their property. The ownership is recorded as a deed. But there are other interests that might provide sufficient control for the purposes of an investment. It is possible to have an option to purchase the property. It is also possible to have a leasehold which provides the ability to use and obtain income from a property without actually owning it. More control is safer and usually provides better tax advantages. Less control may require fewer investment resources while still providing the desired investment returns.

Any real estate investment can be viewed as a change from an existing structure of debt, equity, and control into a new one. We will call the parties who have control of the existing structure the 'sellers'. The person or group who is investing will be called the 'buyers'. The buyers need to know that they can obtain sufficient control from the sellers to meet their objectives. Then they need to figure out how to address the debt and then the equity. There are numerous combinations of approaches on how to address the debt and equity. One of my mentors, Robert Steele, has even written a book, *300 Ways to Buy, Sell, or Exchange Real Estate* (https://www.amazon.com/Steele-Ways-Sell-Exchange-Estate/dp/098951904X) that talks about a large number of creative combinations.

Viewing real estate transactions as debt, equity, and control frees the mind to design creative approaches that can satisfy both the buyers' and the sellers' investment objectives. There are groups of brokers in the U.S. who are dedicated to creative transactions. They call themselves exchangors to emphasize that all real estate sales are exchanges of equity for something else, not just sales for cash. The National Council of Exchangors (NCE) is the most prominent nationwide group that teaches and practices this type of real estate deal-making. The Society of Exchange Counselors (SEC) is another prominent group but is by invitation only.

Selecting Real Estate Investments

When investing in real estate, the investor first takes stock of his objectives, risk tolerance, and resources in terms of time, money, expertise, and assets. An investment deal can come together when the investor's resources are sufficient to address the control, equity, and debt of a seller and replace it with control, equity, and debt from the buyer. The most common and usual deal is where the control of the seller—and later the buyer—is fee simple ownership (full and absolute control of the property). The seller's debt is paid off at closing by a new loan to the buyer. The buyer provides sufficient cash to make up the difference between the property value and the loan amount (usually 20–40% of the property value). The cash that is over and above the payoff of the existing debt goes to the seller for his equity.

Sometimes, none of the standard approaches are used. For example, perhaps the buyer provides a piece of real estate to the seller worth 60% of the value of the seller's property. The seller moves his debt (that happens to be at 40% of the value of his property) to the new property. The buyer provides 20% in cryptocurrency and 20% in a note to the seller secured by the seller's property. In this case, the existing debt is moved. A third of the seller's equity is moved to the buyer's property, another third is provided in a new asset (the cryptocurrency), and the final third is provided by the buyer as a note to be paid off over time.

From the buyer's perspective, he brought to the table 60% of the value in real estate and 20% of the value in cryptocurrency. He ends up with a property that has 20% loan to value debt owed to the seller and has moved the equity he had in his other property plus the equity he had in the cryptocurrency to the new property.

This is only one of many ways to structure deals. I will show you many more as we look at how to buy real estate with cryptocurrency. The key is to remember the debt-equity-control framework and consider alternatives and constraints within any particular deal.

Summary

Real estate investing has always been the principal way to create wealth. Even those who made their initial money in other businesses turn to real estate when they want to build generational wealth. Real estate provides a unique mix of cash flow, appreciation, and tax advantages. But the reliability of real estate to produce returns also means that an investor can leverage and multiply those returns tremendously.

A great way to think about real estate deals is by viewing them as a transfer of debt, equity, and control from the seller to a new framework of debt, equity, and control for the buyer. Thinking of real estate this way frees the investor's mind to invent structures that satisfy everyone's objectives. An investor who thinks this way can close deals that less creative investors can't. The investor who can develop debt, equity, and control structures that fit her resources can also learn to fit cryptocurrency into real estate deals and further improve her returns and her capacity to do more deals.

SECTION II

TRANSFORMING DEAL-MAKING

CHAPTER THREE

HOW CRYPTO WORKS IN SALES AND PURCHASES

T HERE ARE SOME INTERESTING synergies that happen when crypto and real estate are combined. Crypto has been the fastest appreciating asset class over the past five years, blowing away stocks, bonds, real estate, and even much riskier investments. Five years ago, Bitcoin was trading around $320 per coin. As I write this in February 2021, the price is $52,012. That's a 16,253% increase, or an average annual appreciation of 3,250%. Even at its bottom in 2020, Bitcoin was up over 900% during the past five years or 180% annual appreciation. These kind of returns totally eclipse stocks (historical average of ~10% appreciation), and stocks beat everything except properly structured real estate investments. Sophisticated real estate investors target annual returns in the 15%–25% range over the life of the investment.

What I will show you in this section is that the combination of cryptocurrency and real estate may be able to substantially increase real estate returns for real estate investors. And the risk and volatility of cryptocurrency can be mitigated by combining it with the steady growth and cash flow of real estate.

To lay the framework for how to use cryptocurrency in real estate deals, one needs to understand how cryptocurrency is owned, stored, transferred, and used. There is a whole new language that is constantly and rapidly evolving around the use of cryptocurrency. But the basics have steadied, so these terms should still mean what they mean today in a few years. Protecting your investment in cryptocurrency is also important. In this chapter I discuss best practices for protecting and preserving your cryptocurrency assets.

Wallets

Every cryptocurrency is stored and managed using a wallet that acts something like an actual wallet you put money in and something like an account. Wallets are managed by software, and not all wallets can be used for all cryptocurrencies. It is important to ensure that the wallet you use is compatible with the cryptocurrency you will invest in.

You can either access your wallet with a password or a pass phrase (the original wallets used 12-word random pass phrases). It is vital that you remember your password or pass phrase. If you lose it, you'll lose access to your wallet and your cryptocurrency. It is estimated that over a million Bitcoin have been lost forever this way (that's over $50B in value at 2020 prices). This is a case where you want to write down your access information and keep it somewhere safe.

A wallet actually stores a private key that authenticates you as the owner of a public address. When you send or receive cryptocurrency, your public address is the sender or receiver. A wallet can hold multiple addresses. The addresses are long alphanumeric sequences that looks sort of like this:

18QFKbJfLe5dT3QfH7PMF9Zt297Jg1A7C8

There are several types of wallets that can provide different levels of security to your cryptocurrency. Wallets may be "hot"—always on the internet, or "cold"—stored offline and not accessible except when connected to the internet. Wallets can be software or hardware. Hardware wallets look a lot like flash drives that insert into a USB port. When not inserted, they are a form of cold wallet. Some software approaches create your wallet and your private key from your pass phrase when you put the pass phrase into your computer. www.CounterWallet.io is an example of this type of wallet. If you have extremely valuable cryptocurrency, it might be to your advantage to keep a small portion of it in a hot wallet that you can use quickly and easily, and put the rest into a cold wallet that can be safely stored away (possibly even in a safe deposit box at your local bank).

Cryptocurrency Exchanges

Most cryptocurrencies can only be used on a crypto exchange. Think of a crypto exchange as a broker site or a stock market. These websites allow you to exchange your cryptocurrency for another cryptocurrency or even for fiat currency. Usually, these exchanges are very limited. Most will only support a handful of cryptocurrencies (out of thousands). And even within that handful, there are usually only a couple of cryptocurrencies that you can exchange for yours. The cryptocurrencies that can be exchanged for yours are called your **trading pairs**. You can have a wallet without being on an exchange. But you can't be on an exchange unless you have a wallet (though many exchanges will create a wallet for you on their site).

There are two main types of exchanges; centralized and decentralized. Centralized exchanges require you to move your cryptocurrency to a wallet on the exchange in order to trade the crypto. Decentralized exchanges are newer and facilitate you exchanging your crypto with someone else directly from your wallet without the crypto ever actually being on the exchange. The advantages of centralized exchanges are that they are more streamlined and most of the high volume exchanges are centralized. The disadvantage is security. If the exchange is hacked, you could lose your cryptocurrency. Since there is so much cryptocurrency from numerous investors on the exchange, it is an attractive target for hackers. I think that decentralized exchanges will ultimately take over, especially if they can handle many more types of cryptocurrency. But for now, decentralized exchanges can't quite handle the compatibility issues of wallets and tokens.

Much has been made about the privacy of crypto. You are only known as an obscure address in your wallet. In fact, anyone with the passcode can control that wallet. In its early days, the privacy feature was used by criminals to move and launder funds. However, exchanges today perform standard know-your-customer (KYC) and anti-money laundering (AML) checks in order to be on an exchange. Also, you must remember that once a name is tied to a wallet address, every transaction ever done by that address is publicly available and thus can be tied to the name. It's an interesting mix of public transactions tied to private addresses.

There are hundreds of crypto exchanges. A dozen or so are well-known and popular worldwide. Many others are special-purpose exchanges with only a few cryptocurrencies. In 2017 it was relatively easy for a new cryptocurrency to get listed on an exchange, but as crypto proliferated, the exchanges became very choosy and began to charge (sometimes $100,000 or more) to get listed. This selectivity led to the creation of many new exchanges, since thousands of cryptocurrencies were being created and needed a place to trade.

How To Use Cryptocurrency

Now that you have a wallet and a user on one or more exchanges, what exactly do you do with cryptocurrency? The vast majority of investors in cryptocurrency do exactly three things: they buy it, they hold it hoping it will go up in value, and they exchange it for another cryptocurrency or fiat. That's it. Buy, sell, hold. That's about what most people do with stocks and bonds, too. And, to be frank, that's what too many real estate investors do, too. But there are numerous other ways to use cryptocurrency that should be in our toolbox when we begin to connect crypto and real estate.

Crypto is an asset. And anything you can do with an asset, you can do with crypto. That means an investor can use the value of crypto as security for a loan. In fact, crypto can itself be loaned, pledged, or hypothecated. Admittedly, there are fewer avenues to date to use crypto this way, but as crypto gets more accepted, more companies and individuals will accept cryptocurrency as security. Currently there are lenders who will lend against cryptocurrency. Typically, loans are at 50% loan to value. There is risk in using cryptocurrency this way. If the value drops, there may be a margin call where the lender wants either the loan repaid or additional security. These are the same issues faced by those who take out loans secured by stocks.

While you can use cryptocurrency as security for a loan where you are the borrower, you can also provide the cryptocurrency as security for other parties. It can secure their loans or be used to bolster their assets, often in exchange for a percentage or a fee. In one example, a large insurance company rented cryptocurrency to increase its assets that are held against the insurance policies. Renting the cryptocurrency allowed the insurance company to write more policies. In another case, crypto was borrowed as an asset to increase the balance sheet for buyers of a major sports team. Both of these examples are from TROPTIONS tokens.

Some cryptocurrencies are now accepted for payment at a number of retailers. Bitcoin is accepted at over 70,000 retailers. There are cryptocurrency ATMs. There are credit and debit cards just now beginning to be used that allow payment with crypto. PayPal has just created its own crypto exchange that will allow payments via PayPal to be made with cryptocurrency and Master-Card has just announced that it will be handling cryptocurrencies later in 2021. The mechanics of how payments are made vary depending on the activity and the cryptocurrency. In many cases, payment is made by selling the cryptocurrency on an exchange and paying cash. But a rising number of transaction types support transferring the cryptocurrency directly. As I will show you later in this book, accepting cryptocurrency for payments within your real estate business can be a competitive advantage.

Another thing you can do with cryptocurrency is to send it to another party. Once you exchange crypto for another crypto or fiat, your cryptocurrency is sent to another wallet, and what you traded for is sent to yours. But you can unilaterally send cryptocurrency to another wallet. This is the usual process when you trade for assets outside of an exchange. You send them crypto and they 'send' you their car, their real estate, their jewelry, or other asset.

Using Cryptocurrency in Real Estate Investing

The simplest way to use cryptocurrency in real estate investing is to just buy real estate with cryptocurrency (more on this in Chapter 6). You give the seller the cryptocurrency, and they give you the real estate. While the concept is simple, the execution may not be (see Chapter 7). Several modifications can be made to this straight-purchase process. Cryptocurrency can be used as the down payment, with the rest of the purchase being paid in cash or with a loan. Another option might be to use cryptocurrency as the deposit for a sale (either refundable or not). This approach gives the real estate investor more time to put together a more traditional purchase structure.

There are also a number of approaches that use cryptocurrency as collateral for a loan. If the investor can get a loan secured by cryptocurrency, the loan proceeds could be used in a real estate purchase. This approach leaves the real estate free and clear, and the income from the real estate can pay the loan payments. As an alternative, cryptocurrency can be used as additional collateral for a loan that is primarily secured by real estate. The additional collateral could improve loan terms and increase loan to value for the real estate loan. Lastly, the huge benefit of cryptocurrency—the massive appreciation that has happened for many crypto—gives an investor a stronger balance sheet that can help in sponsoring real estate deals and qualifying for loans even if the loans are largely supported by the real estate deals.

All of these basic techniques for using cryptocurrency in real estate investing rely on the mechanics I discussed earlier in this chapter—creating wallets and buying, selling, holding, or transferring the cryptocurrency using an exchange. Using these basic tools, I will show you specifically how to structure real estate deals to provide win-win solutions for buyers and sellers.

Summary

Cryptocurrency has been the fastest appreciating asset in history. The returns are phenomenal. Just in the past few months Bitcoin has more than tripled, and Ethereum is at a new all-time high.

Crypto is easy to use but sophisticated in its privacy and security. You hold cryptocurrency in wallets that implement public key cryptography and trade cryptocurrency on a variety of crypto exchanges. As crypto becomes more mainstream, it is getting even easier to use. PayPal and MasterCard are implementing methods to pay vendors with cryptocurrency. And these efforts are just the beginning.

To use cryptocurrency in real estate is also straightforward: you send the crypto to the seller and the seller signs over the deed. As we will see, there are potential complications in such a transaction, but it is simple at its core.

CHAPTER FOUR

BARTER CRYPTOCURRENCY

W HILE CRYPTOCURRENCY HAS A lot of potential for use in real estate deals, there is a type of cryptocurrency that may be best to use. Barter cryptocurrency, crypto specifically created for bartering transactions, has the right mix of capabilities to make it especially appropriate for real estate transactions. To understand the potential uses of barter cryptocurrency, it is important to understand how barter transactions are carried out in the 21st century.

Barter is the direct exchange of goods and/or services. I give you five TVs and you give me a dishwasher. Or I do your taxes and you set up my Wi-Fi. It's the same as before money existed and before the use of gold as an intermediary.

Barter currency makes that exchange one step removed. A lawyer can exchange future hours for barter currency and then use that currency to buy the services of a plumber. It's sort of like money in that way, but it is usually a closed ecosystem. The value of the barter currency is what is accepted between the parties. Often the issuer of a barter currency acts as a clearinghouse and takes a small percentage of the trade to facilitate it. Alternatively, the currency issuer may charge a small premium over the perceived value of using the barter currency when the currency is obtained, and then the barter itself may be at the value of the barter currency.

If barter currency acts a lot like money, why not just use fiat money? After all, fiat money is extremely liquid and as such can be used to buy any services or goods really. What are the advantages of barter currency?

Advantages and Disadvantages of Barter Currency

There are a number of transactions that fiat money is just not suited for. How can a lawyer sell future hours, a hotel offer future rooms, or a farmer promise future crops for money? In some cases, factor loans can be used for future receivables, but these loans are typically very expensive on top of the certain devaluation of the fiat currency itself. In essence, for these types of transactions, you pay a premium for the liquidity advantage of fiat currency. If barter currency is liquid enough for your purposes, using it can be a substantial advantage.

Barter currency is not denominated in fiat currency. A barter dollar is not necessarily pegged to a U.S. dollar. This means that when the dollar devalues, barter currency does not necessarily follow. Not being denominated in fiat has other potential advantages for barter currency. Foremost among those is a great deal of flexibility in valuing transactions. If you essentially trade an hour of legal services for two hours of plumbing services, is that worth $100 in fiat? $200 in fiat? $50 in fiat? Using barter currency may mean that only the ratio of costs is certain, not the absolute costs. This feature provides flexibility in the recognition of income and expenses for businesses. Keeping the ratios the same also preserves purchasing power which using fiat does not.

There are numerous barter currency groups that have been created over the years. Among the largest is the International Trade Exchange (ITEX) group that has tens of thousands of participants. A barter group is as good as the size of its market. The more people involved, the greater the value of the barter currency because it enables the participants to use the currency for more trades.

A downside of barter currency is the potential for forgery. Barter currency issuers don't have the same resources that a country has to create notes that can't be forged. And electronic barter currency has the same susceptibility to hackers that any electronic site has.

A further downside is that online barter currency sites are single websites that must be marketed and maintained by the issuer, and all the exchange mechanisms must also be created and maintained by the issuer. There is no infrastructure beyond that developed by the issuer to expand the market or maintain the integrity of the barter currency. One could ask what happens when a barter currency goes out of business? It may be that the currency loses all value.

Barter Cryptocurrency

Barter cryptocurrency solves many of the problems with barter currency while maintaining all of the advantages. Crypto can still be issued flexibly so that participants can promise goods or services in exchange for it. It is still possible to value the cryptocurrency as an asset rather than denominated in U.S. dollars when trading the crypto for an asset or service. But barter crypto on the blockchain cannot be readily forged and, especially if the crypto transactions are recorded on a popular public blockchain, the crypto will still be usable even if the original issuer disappears or goes out of business. If the crypto increases in value, it can be subdivided to continue supporting smaller transactions.

Barter crypto is also easy to trade internationally (just as all cryptocurrency is), so it can be used globally with no difficulties. And those trades may be accomplished using normal crypto exchanges rather than specialized barter sites (though as we will see, it may be very desirable for specialized barter sites to exist either instead of or in conjunction with crypto exchanges).

Putting barter currency on the blockchain is really a marriage made in heaven. The blockchain provides the infrastructure that a barter currency needs. The barter currency provides a capability and an approach that increases the potential uses of blockchain.

There is one substantial hurdle for barter cryptocurrency to overcome, however. This has to do with valuing the cryptocurrency. The way crypto is designed, its value is determined by its trading pairs on a crypto exchange. This means that the only way for an independent party to assess the value of the crypto is to look at trades of the crypto for other crypto or for fiat. But barter crypto is designed to be traded directly for assets. For example, I send you 1,000 XTROPTIONS.GOLD and you sign over title to your car. It is recorded on the blockchain that 1,000 XTROPTIONS.GOLD were sent from one wallet to another —with no implication of the value of the crypto in that trade. When the vast majority of trades using barter cryptocurrency are of this sort, there is very little information for someone to use in assessing what value to ask for the cryptocurrency. This lack of information also tends to depress the market for the cryptocurrency because some people (especially for larger transactions) will be uncomfortable assigning any value to the cryptocurrency.

This valuation hurdle is the primary reason that barter crypto has not yet taken off in a similar fashion to Bitcoin. The most likely solution is for barter crypto issuers to create marketplaces similar to what barter currency providers have done. Those marketplaces will facilitate transactions and augment the valuation capability that is already present from trades for other crypto or fiat. If a marketplace is created where, for example, I can trade 10 XTROPTIONS. GOLD for a blender with an imputed value of $50 retail (making each XTROPTIONS.GOLD valued at $5), that trade can be used as additional information to assess the value of the cryptocurrency.

TROPTIONS

Two existing tokens that are designed for barter are the TROPTIONS suite of tokens and the REXNET network of tokens. TROPTIONS, which is short for 'trade options', were originally created in 2003 and registered as a digital currency with the SEC in 2004. (This was long before the creation of Bitcoin). It was a way of trading different kinds of options using an intermediate asset. It's a form of derivatives, but it acts a lot like a barter currency. But while the digital currency existed, there were no good mechanisms for managing it. In 2016, the founder of TROPTIONS, Garland Harris, had the brilliant idea to take this idea of a barter dollar and to put it onto the blockchain. The possibility for fraud and counterfeit dollars went away. The potential for double spending went away. Transactions were now immutable, known, international, and easy to do; it was a huge advance on barter currency.

The blockchain version of TROPTIONS started off with 'TROPTIONS' in 2016. Subsequently, there were several hard and soft forks (forks are when a cryptocurrency changes names—hard fork—or splits into two tokens with each of the holders getting both—soft fork) so that now there's a whole suite of tokens: XTROPTIONS, XTROPTIONS.GOLD, XTROPTIONS.AUS, and TROPTIONS.GOLD. Those are the ones that are traded most often now. As a shortcut, I will call all the tokens TROPTIONS, but I mean any of the individual tokens.

How do you use TROPTIONS if you want to trade directly for an asset? Suppose you want to trade TROPTIONS for a car. What happens on the blockchain is not that you trade TROPTIONS for a car; there isn't yet a way of documenting the car side of this transaction. Instead, the person signs over the title of the car and you send the TROPTIONS to the person who owned the car. All you see on the blockchain is the send of TROPTIONS from one wallet to another.

TROPTIONS are intended to be traded as tokens for assets, so it's very easy to do that directly. You just have the person who has the asset create a wallet and you send them the tokens. They give you the asset. It's very simple, but that doesn't get recorded on the blockchain. Only the send gets recorded. Then the value of the transaction (by which I mean the notional value of how many fiat dollars you thought the car was worth and how many fiat dollars you thought the TROPTIONS were worth) disappears. It's not recorded anywhere; the information can't be mined, and it can't be used very easily in order to determine the price of the token.

That is a downside to using barter currencies for cryptocurrency exchange, but it also points to a lack that can be filled by software; software could be created to capture the agreement between the person with the asset and the person with the TROPTIONS. There's no reason why that information can't be documented as a smart contract on a blockchain and the values then mined.

There are some reasons why not all people doing these types of transactions would want the exact value of the asset or tokens to be known. If you trade an asset for an asset, the IRS tells you that you are supposed to establish the value of the assets in fiat currency so that you can calculate your gain or loss in the asset and report it as income (loss) in your tax return. This is very easy if you trade real estate for dollars. If you buy a house for $100,000, the house has a basis (all things being equal) of $100,000, and if you sell it for

$120,000, you have a gain of $20,000 (assuming no changes to the basis or deductions from the price). However, if you buy a house for $100,000 and trade it for a flex warehouse, what was the value of the trade? The IRS prefers that you identify a dollar value you would have sold it for and set that as the price on both sides of the trade. In reality, this value is whatever is agreed between the buyer and seller and could realistically span a rather wide range. The flexibility in identifying the exchange price is an advantage to doing asset-for-asset swaps.

There are some who argue that trading an asset for an asset is not a taxable event because there is no ability to accurately fix a dollar value to the trade. I have heard accountants espouse both sides of this argument and, not being an accountant or being qualified to dispense accounting advice, I will not weigh in.

Why would a seller consider accepting TROPTIONS instead of cash for their property? That's an important question, and it goes back to the discussion about property exchange. Nobody really wants cash; everybody wants what cash will buy them. What a real estate seller will want is what the cryptocurrency could buy them or achieve for them.

What are some of the things that cryptocurrency could achieve for the seller that cash won't? First, cryptocurrency can go up in value, whereas we know that all of the fiat currencies will go down in value. Fiat currency goes down in value at about 2 to 3% per year by decree because that's what the various federal reserve banks want. They manage 'official' inflation to be 2 to 3% per year, knowing that the purchasing power of your cash is going to go down every single year (but making it easier to repay national debt with cheaper currency). Thus, you know that the value of what you received for your property will go down every year.

On the other hand, if you accept cryptocurrency for your property, that cryptocurrency may actually go up in value. If you were getting $1,000,000 in cash and instead you got $1,000,000 in cryptocurrency, the crypto might be worth $2,000,000 or $10,000,000 in a short period of time based on how cryptocurrency has performed over the past few years. There is the risk as well that the cryptocurrency could go down in value or crash.

If you really don't want the cash—you want what the cash will buy you—then crypto might be a strong place to hold your proceeds short-term. Crypto can act as an investment itself with the easy potential to appreciate substantially. As long as you can move the crypto to another investment, you may find that the combination of crypto and real estate has a return multiplier.

For example, if you sell your million-dollar building for $500,000 in cash and $500,000 equivalent in crypto, you may find that by the time you are reinvesting in a new property, the $500,000 in crypto has become worth $750,000. Now you have $1,250,000 to invest in a new property. Using 75% leverage (75% of the new property will be a loan), you can now get a $5M property, where if you had used only cash you would be able to get a $4M property. This synergy of using crypto for appreciation and real estate to consolidate those gains is a key reason to use barter cryptocurrency.

International real estate purchases also face challenges moving money across country borders. I've heard numerous examples of people trying to move money into the United States in order to close on a real estate transaction and that money being held up by the Treasury Department or by other organizations as they go through their KYC and AML procedures. In some cases, money has been held up for months, if not years, and the projects fell apart because the money couldn't be moved across the borders. With cryptocurrency there is no impediment to moving across borders whatsoever; it's a simple exchange on a website that is outside of any country's jurisdiction.

Another reason you might accept cryptocurrency is to allow you to manage the value of the transaction. If you sell for cash, you know exactly what the value of the cash is. If you sell for cryptocurrency, there is some flexibility in how you allocate the value of your property and the value of the cryptocurrency, and maybe even opportunity to manage capital gains for your property. This would be true in any sort of asset-for-asset exchange. For example, in the original 1031 exchange where people traded property for property, you might trade your house for my apartment complex and a note. The value of the house and the value of the apartment complex are relative. There's a range of reasonable values that could be set for that transaction.

Similarly, for cryptocurrency the value that the seller gets for the crypto might be the value that's currently published on xchain.io. It might be the value based on peer-to-peer exchanges. Or it might be a discounted value because of the volatility of the cryptocurrency or due to some other factor in the exchange. Any of those values might be reasonable ones to use in a particular transaction. The use of cryptocurrency provides a greater degree of creativity and flexibility in the transaction itself.

TROPTIONS, in particular, has a strong history of actually being used in transactions. It has been used to purchase millions of dollars of real estate, possibly more than any other cryptocurrency (including Bitcoin) when you look at direct exchange of crypto for real estate. TROPTIONS have directly purchased dozens of cars, jewelry, and services like cellphone contracts and dental work. TROPTIONS may be the strongest candidate for a barter currency.

TROPTIONS have also appreciated substantially since their inception. For example, XTROPTIONS.GOLD started at $.10. From there they increased to ~$120.00. At that time, the issuers decided to distribute additional tokens at a 1200-to-1 ratio (essentially like a stock split of 1200 to 1), driving the price back down to $.10. Since then, the price has risen again to around $4.00, making the current price approximately 48,000 times the initial price over the course of two and a half years. Other TROPTIONS tokens have also appreciated substantially over the course of their trading.

REXNET

Real Estate Exchange Network (REXNET) has an interesting approach to barter. They create a 'Haves/Wants' board (an approach taken from the real estate exchange industry). A Haves/Wants board is like a series of classified ads. Each posting tells what the poster has (I have a 25 unit apartment complex for sale) and what they want (I want to sell it for $2,500,000 and will accept cryptocurrency for 25% of the purchase price).

REXNET also creates a network of tokens that can be interchanged but have specific focus within a geographic area or industry (for example, REXNET.Panama or REXNET.baseball) in addition to their flagship REXNET token. This approach creates a network of crypto issuers that work together to make each token more useful and more valuable.

REXNET also takes an alternative approach to valuation that works well within a barter environment. Bitcoin uses 'proof of work' as its basis of value, and other coins and tokens use 'proof of stake.' REXNET uses 'proof of use.' The value of REXNET increases for every million tokens sent as part of a validated exchange. Thus, the more the tokens are sent in trade, the greater the value. And the value is predictable—essentially no volatility—and increases over time. Proof of use is a clever approach to addressing the valuation problem with barter currencies. It is especially effective when a token is new because it supports the price and provides confidence in the distribution of tokens. The value is obtained just from cryptocurrency sends. It isn't necessary to put the entire transaction on the blockchain in order to determine value.

As of early 2021, the full infrastructure for REXNET is in development. The founders plan to implement a robust REXNET Listings Service that is inspired by some of the largest names in internet shopping and modeled after a mature real estate exchange approach. The service anticipates incorporating smart contracts to facilitate the cryptocurrency-for-real-estate transactions. This online marketplace will be paired with exchange meetings focused on international real estate that will assist with the marketing and deal flow for the tokens. Once the full suite of capabilities is in place, REXNET will have a complete approach to using barter currency in real estate deals. It will have a marketplace to match buyers and sellers, transaction support via smart contracts, and a firm foundation for valuation of the tokens. This new token is one to watch.

These two types of barter tokens represent the main approaches where the tokens themselves are used for barter assets and not as utility tokens to facilitate direct exchanges. New approaches could potentially emerge; given the innovative nature of crypto, that will almost certainly happen. For now, TROPTIONS and REXNET represent the best in barter currency. They are both good candidates to use in deals for real estate or other assets.

Summary

Barter currency and now barter cryptocurrency provide a unique approach to exchanging assets. Barter currencies can act like money. They can act as intermediary stores of value between trades. But they don't automatically devalue like currencies; they are a better store of value. There can be challenges in liquidity, however, since any particular barter currency will not be as widely used as fiat.

Barter cryptocurrencies solve many of the critical flaws in barter currency. They eliminate the potential for counterfeiting or double spending and provide mechanisms for storing and exchanging the currencies through the blockchain.

TROPTIONS was the original barter cryptocurrency and has been used in more asset-for-asset transactions than any cryptocurrency, with the possible exception of Bitcoin. TROPTIONS have been used for large real estate transactions and numerous purchases of cars, jewelry, and other assets. TROPTIONS have even been featured on NASCAR cars with the sponsorship paid for in the cryptocurrency.

REXNET is another interesting approach to barter cryptocurrency. Its network of barter tokens can become an entire barter ecosystem if it is appropriately scaled and managed.

Barter cryptocurrencies have a unique place in the intersection of real estate and cryptocurrency and may become the primary methods for real estate exchanges for crypto. These crypto assets are ones to watch as cryptocurrency and real estate become intertwined.

CHAPTER FIVE

REAL ESTATE DEAL STRUCTURES

TO INJECT CRYPTOCURRENCY IN the mix of real estate deals, you have to be able to structure real estate deals that make it possible to use cryptocurrency. The vast majority of real estate deals done in the U.S., however, follow a single simple formula. Provide a down payment in cash and obtain a loan secured by a mortgage against the real estate. The amount of the loan is usually 65% to 80% of the price of the property. For many investors and for a disappointing number of real estate brokers, that is the only way to purchase properties.

That approach is conventional and works well when:

- the seller has a property that appraises for the purchase price
- the buyer has the down payment in cash (whether her own or raised from investors)
- the credit markets are operating normally
- interest rates are lower than capitalization rates

- and the buyer (or her team) has a net worth that is more than the loan amount.

Those conditions are in place often enough that many real estate transactions are completed.

When Standard Conditions Fail

But what about when the conditions are not met? Most investors have been around long enough to remember the real estate crash in the late 2000s. Many of the conditions above—led by the seizing of the credit markets—failed to materialize. Investors who could not compensate in some way could not do deals and could not even refinance their properties when loans came due. Properties failed to appraise. Loans were not available. And the net worth of many buyers took a substantial hit. As I write this in the year 2020, there are similar challenges due to the Covid-19 pandemic. Whether they will result in longer term damage to the real estate market is yet to be determined. So far, markets have remained hot, though there have been additional requirements and restrictions on lending, like a requirement for additional escrow accounts for commercial mortgages.

In times of upheaval or even just downturns of the business cycle, it can be advantageous to property sellers who want to close a deal or to buyers who don't meet the ideal profile to have alternative approaches to structuring real estate deals. Flexible buyers and sellers can still close deals beneficial to each other when more stodgy counterparties are stalled. But they have to know how to use those alternative approaches to structure deals.

There is an implicit assumption in the standard deal structure that the seller's objective is to get the highest price and the buyer's objective is to get a lower price. However, this is rarely the case.

Sometimes a seller prefers a quick sale. Sometimes a seller needs to defer capital gains. Often, the seller is really looking to move up and buy a bigger property. The standard deal structure ignores all these objectives. The only bargaining point is really price. Sometimes price is enough to make the deal good enough for the buyer and seller. But by deliberately taking into account other objectives, there are often ways of making a deal work that are better than just setting a slightly different price.

Earlier I pointed out that flexible deal structures are created by moving the seller's debt, equity, and control structure into a buyer's debt, equity, and control structure. The types of resources needed depend on the objectives of the buyer and seller. But they also depend on counterparty requirements. A counterparty is, in this case, anyone who has to approve the deal besides the buyer and seller. The most common counterparties are lenders, brokers, and investors. A lender may have to approve a loan or agree to an assumption. A broker may have to agree to alternative forms of commission like a note or equity in the project. And investors must agree to commit their funds. Naturally, the fewer counterparties involved, the easier it is to negotiate a deal. When the only deciding parties are the buyer and the seller, there are numerous deal structures that can be created. When the decision makers are counterparties who have no particular interest in making the deal, structuring any deal may be challenging. Most commercial real estate investors have been frustrated at one point or another with an 'advisor' who kills the deal because he or she just didn't care if the deal went through but would have been blamed if a bad deal was done.

Alternative Deal Structures

There are some alternative approaches that are more common than others in structuring real estate deals. One of these is to incorporate seller financing. Sometimes the seller will be the lender in first position (having the senior lien against the property). Sometimes a seller will hold a mortgage behind another lender (in second position) to bridge between the loan amount and the buyer's down payment. There are more creative approaches as well. Sellers can wrap a mortgage—keep the existing mortgage in place while securing a larger mortgage for the buyer. Or a seller can allow a buyer to obtain the property 'subject to' an existing mortgage.

When both the buyer and seller own property, there are many ways to incorporate additional property into a deal. The buyer can provide a property as a down payment instead of cash. Properties can be swapped. (This, by the way, was the original 1031 tax deferred exchange). Or another property could be the security for a seller mortgage. Using another property as collateral is especially useful if a lender will not allow a seller second to be placed on the property being purchased. A buyer property could be used as collateral (or as additional collateral) for a third-party lender. When it is used as additional collateral, the loan is said to be cross-collateralized.

To make a project more attractive to a buyer, sellers can offer to lease back the property or to buy it back at some future date. It may be possible to guarantee rent (especially if necessary to satisfy a lender that the property can cover the debt). Sellers can also offer to assist with management or tenant acquisition.

Once minds are opened to the many alternative deal structuring approaches between a buyer and a seller, it may also be possible to incorporate third parties who provide some asset or capability that completes the deal. This approach can lead to multi-leg property exchanges. For example, suppose A has a small apartment complex he wants to sell. B wants the apartment complex and has some cash and a few buildable lots in a desirable subdivision. C is a developer who would be interested in building on the lots and has a commercial building he just completed and is trying to sell. No two of these people could make a deal. A doesn't want B's lots. C doesn't want A's apartment complex. But if B takes the apartment complexes, A takes the commercial building and C takes B's lots, a deal may be structured that satisfies everyone's objectives.

Property Exchange

It is relatively straightforward to make a three-way transaction between willing buyers/sellers. But the process of finding a third party to complete a transaction is one that has been perfected by the property-exchange community. And it can be extended. Four-way, five-way, etc. transactions are regularly completed. Rumor has it that the record is a 42-leg transaction, though that does stretch the bounds of credulity.

To show the power of exchanging, there is a true story of a man who began exchanging with a red paper clip and ended up with a house. The entire story including details of each individual transaction can be seen online. It took a total of 14 transactions. He first traded the paperclip for a fish-shaped pen. Then he traded the pen for a hand-sculpted doorknob. In many cases he traded for services (an instant party, a movie role, a recording contract). At each stage, both parties of the transaction were happy to trade and gained benefits from the trade. If at every transaction both parties denominated their property in dollars and traded for price, none of these transactions would have happened. But since the unique features of what was being exchanged had different values to the different traders, the exchanges were not only possible, but desirable for each party. (The whole video is available here: https://www.youtube.com/watch?v=8s3bdVxuFBs).

Currency in Exchanges

Currency has a very special role within exchanges. It is the most liquid of assets, which is why the standard approach focuses solely on currency. But within property exchanges it is often currency that makes up the difference in property values. If one property is worth about $1,000,000 and the other is worth around $750,000, even accounting for the values to buyer and seller being somewhat different, it is likely that the owner of the million-dollar property will want something in addition to the other property in the exchange. In this case, we say that the money is used to balance the equities.

There are, however, several types of currency. Really anything that can be readily subdivided into small amounts and that can be sold easily can act as currency. The most well-known is fiat currency: dollar, euros, yuan, etc. It can be used for transactions in almost any amount and is universally accepted. A second type of currency is physical. Precious metals, especially gold or silver coins, can be used as currency to fill in the gaps in a transaction and are also readily accepted or can quickly be sold to purchase anything. A third type of currency is currency land. These are usually small, inexpensive plots of land that can act as a store of value and be traded in real estate transactions. Currency land is often used in real estate exchanges and is not as well known outside those circles. The last type of currency is cryptocurrency. As a digital currency, it is easily sold or traded. It is more subdividable than even fiat currency. It has fewer restrictions on movement and is (so far) less regulated than fiat.

All of these currencies are useful in real estate deals, but different types better support different types of transactions. When flexibility in valuation is desired, currency land and cryptocurrency are preferred. If immediate liquidity is necessary, nothing beats fiat currency. For international transactions, cryptocurrency is much simpler to use and much easier to transfer. When a seller wants something that seems more substantial, currency land or gold are good options. And if a seller wants limited risk, currency land wins. Cryptocurrency has a good deal of risk in value and liquidity (as well as potential upside). Fiat will certainly devalue if held for any length of time, and prices of gold and other physical currency can fluctuate substantially. Currency land, on the other hand, has little fluctuation in value, can't be lost or stolen, and lasts forever. Each currency has its place.

Currency land is one useful technique among many to support structuring property exchange deals. And viewing deals from the lens of property exchange creates many more opportunities to construct a deal that supports both the buyer and the seller—especially when there are conditions that don't allow for the standard deal structure. Property exchange is often necessary during market declines or collapses. Those seem to happen about every 10 years nowadays. But using these techniques may be vital when the buyer doesn't fit the standard deal criteria. And these approaches may be far more beneficial for a seller whose primary objective isn't price. In short, these approaches are likely to be better than the standard deal for a majority of transactions.

Summary

The most common approach to structuring a deal is also an approach that is vulnerable to market conditions. Lack of credit markets or properties, buyers, or sellers who are in some way imperfect can all derail a deal between a willing buyer and seller.

Fortunately, there are many alternative ways to structure a deal. The discipline of property exchange provides a framework of methods to ensure a deal closes. Seller notes, trading properties, multi-leg exchanges, and the use of additional asset types can all be combined to create deals that satisfy everyone's objectives. As long as buyers, sellers, and the other parties involved in a deal can be flexible and act in their own best interest, deals can be closed even when they don't fit the usual parameters.

Currency has a special place in deal structures. It fills the gaps and smooths the process. But there are several types of currency in addition to fiat. Physical currency, currency land, and cryptocurrency have different properties and can be used to address different needs in deal structures. Cryptocurrency especially can be easily moved internationally, and its dramatic upside can make it an attractive component to close a deal.

CHAPTER SIX

STRUCTURES AND EXAMPLES FOR CRYPTO – REAL ESTATE EXCHANGES

N OW THAT YOU UNDERSTAND the advantages and disadvantages of cryptocurrency and how flexible deals can be structured, I will walk you through a few cryptocurrency deal structures. All of these approaches combine real estate and cryptocurrency. For the most part, I describe them from the perspective of a buyer with cryptocurrency wanting to purchase real estate.

As you will remember from previous chapters, real estate deals are structured by debt, equity, and control. The techniques themselves vary depending on what type of control is needed. The vast majority of real estate deals are done where title is exchanged, so I will start with those.

Techniques When Title is Exchanged

Suppose that a transfer of title to the real estate is the control desired in the transaction. In these deals, we have to address existing and new debt and we have to address what the seller receives for her equity. The debt is usually handled first.

Cryptocurrency and Debt

Strategy 1: Loan against cryptocurrency

The first technique is using cryptocurrency as security for a loan. Using this technique, you would obtain a loan secured by your cryptocurrency, just as you might obtain a loan secured by a brokerage account that has equities (stocks). You'd use this technique for many of the same reasons you would use it for a brokerage account. If you sell stocks or your cryptocurrency, you may trigger a capital gains tax; if you take a loan secured by the crypto, there is no tax consequence (in the U.S.). Further, in the case of a desirable cryptocurrency that is appreciating, you gain the advantage of the crypto appreciation by taking out a loan instead of selling it. You continue to make return on the cryptocurrency while the loan is in place.

There is a risk here as well. If the cryptocurrency depreciates, you may have a margin call. If the value of the cryptocurrency falls below a threshold, the lender will ask you to increase the amount of the security. Given the volatility of cryptocurrency, it may be desirable to use lower leverage (a lower loan to value) on the cryptocurrency to provide some contingency in the case of a downturn.

This approach is one of the easiest ways to use cryptocurrency for a real estate deal. You need to find a lender who will loan against your crypto, but the number of lenders who will do that is rapidly increasing. Within the next few years, it will become common. But once you have the loan, you are buying the real estate with cash— the easiest deals to make. This cash may be used for the down payment or as the total purchase price. Using it as a down payment gives you double leverage (you have a loan against the crypto and a loan against the property), but the combined loan payments may still be a cheaper cost of capital than having investors provide the down payment funds.

Cost of capital is a key consideration in real estate investing and one everyone should be very aware of when using cryptocurrency. When purchasing a property, every investor must compare the income and other returns from owning the property with the costs of the funds and/or assets used in the purchase. In the case of obtaining a loan against crypto to use to purchase real estate, you should ask several questions and use the answers to make tradeoffs for your investment decisions:

- What will the capital cost you during the investment? You should count the loan closing costs, any points charged at the beginning or end of the loan, and the interest due during the loan term. Usually these costs divide into one-time costs that are figured at the beginning or end and debt service costs. You have to know what income you receive and when you receive it in order to service debt.
- What income will the real estate provide you during the loan term? From this income you can calculate a debt service coverage ratio (DSCR) calculated as income/debt service. Most lenders like to see a DSCR above 1.25, but higher DSCRs may be required for riskier projects.
- What return is acceptable to you given the risk and time-frame of the deal?

The simplest way to look at these questions is that the income provided by the property minus the debt service should be greater than the return you need to make the deal interesting.

Income – Debt Service > Desired Return

The cost of capital is a vital factor in deciding whether a particular deal structure makes sense.

The usual ways of obtaining capital are either to already have it, to sell investments that have appreciated, to borrow it, or to partner with others who have capital, generally providing them equity (ownership) in the project and a good return. Of these alternatives, the cost of capital varies greatly. Capital you already have or that can be obtained by selling other investments has no direct cost, only opportunity cost (the cost of what you would have received if you had kept the investments or used the money in an alternative investment). But loans have a real cost between interest and points that can range from the low single digit percentages to the mid-teens for hard money loans. And equity investors typically look for double digit returns on their investments.

In doing this overall calculation, then, obtaining a loan against your cryptocurrency probably has a greater cost of capital than a loan against real estate. But it has a lower cost of capital than taking on an equity investor or than selling the cryptocurrency and both paying capital gains taxes and losing the continued appreciation of the cryptocurrency.

Strategy 2: Cross-collateralization

I introduced cross-collateralization in an earlier chapter. It involved using another real estate asset or another type of asset to provide additional collateral and obtain a larger loan against the property being purchased. With this technique, the cryptocurrency is used along with real estate to secure a loan. All the benefits I discussed in the first strategy above are also benefits here. The cryptocurrency is not sold or transferred, so there are no tax implications, and any appreciation is also retained. However, there are nuances to cross-collateralization that affect deal structure and timing.

One cross-collateralization approach is to add real estate as additional security to a cryptocurrency loan. You may get better terms on a cryptocurrency loan if the real estate you purchase with the loan proceeds is also added as security to a cryptocurrency loan. This tactic may give a lender more confidence in making the cryptocurrency loan, knowing that in addition to the crypto, they will have a more traditional hard asset as collateral.

Alternatively, you could obtain a real estate loan and provide cryptocurrency as additional collateral. In both cases you have mixed collateral, but in the first case you are getting a crypto loan and adding real estate. In the second case you are getting a traditional real estate loan and adding another asset, cryptocurrency, as additional security. This is usually done to increase the loan to value of the real estate loan and will still rely on the property income being sufficient to satisfy the debt service.

Strategy 3: Lending cryptocurrency

It is also possible to be the lender rather than the borrower. If you lend your cryptocurrency to another you may be paid interest in cash that can be used to augment real estate income or fund acquisitions. Why would someone want to borrow your cryptocurrency? One TROPTIONS holder lent his TROPTIONS to an insurance company so they could have additional assets on their books and be enabled to write additional insurance policies. Any organization that is required to have assets in reserve may desire to rent assets to make up any shortfall in their reserves or increase their capacity to do business.

Specific properties or uses of a cryptocurrency may also prompt someone to borrow a particular cryptocurrency. If one cryptocurrency is preferred on a particular crypto exchange, it may be useful to have quantities of that crypto rather than another or rather than fiat. Also, many cryptocurrencies are based on a particular technology or have unusual uses that may provide a substantial advantage. In those cases, the person who needs the cryptocurrency may borrow it. There are substantial challenges in borrowing cryptocurrency. Generally, the immutability of a transaction is a positive factor for cryptocurrency. And usually the lack of specific crypto regulations facilitates doing business. The downside to immutable transactions is that they can't be reversed. The downside to a lack of regulation is that there is no authority that can get the crypto back for you if you loan it out and the borrower defaults. However, as crypto has become more mainstream, there are third-party escrow agents who could hold the cryptocurrency for a loan and mitigate these risks.

A second approach to lending cryptocurrency is to lend part crypto and part cash. I must credit Bob Steele for pioneering this approach with the REXNET cryptocurrency. Bob is a brilliant deal-making strategist for real estate. In this case, the lender lends a loan amount with some fraction of fiat currency and crypto. The sweet spot in the market seems to be a mix of 75% cash and 25% crypto. For example, a borrower borrows $2,000,000 and receives the funds as $1,500,000 in cash and the equivalent of $500,000 in cryptocurrency. Interest is paid on the full $2,000,000 and the loan is ultimately repaid in dollars. The borrower keeps the cryptocurrency.

Why would a lender want to make such a loan? Some cryptocurrencies are less liquid than others. Making this loan converts some of the lender's cryptocurrency to an income stream and ultimately converts the crypto to cash. Lending the money and the crypto achieves the investor's objectives of liquidity for some of his crypto.

Why would a borrower borrow $2,000,000 when they only need the $1,500,000 cash? Remember that an investor must evaluate the income from the property minus the cost of capital to assess her return. In many cases, a $2,000,000 loan would still be cheaper cost of capital than a hard money loan or an equity investor. Further, if the cryptocurrency increases in value and can be sold or used in another project, the cryptocurrency could allow the investor to pay back the entire loan. The combination of these factors can make such a loan extremely attractive to a borrower.

Strategy 4: Qualifying for a loan

This strategy involves using cryptocurrency to help qualify for a loan. When a lender decides to make a commercial loan, it is customary to require the borrowers to qualify along at least three criteria to get the loan. First, the borrower (or their team) must have a net worth equal to the loan amount. Second, the borrower should have liquidity of six months to a year of loan payments outside the income of the property. Third, the borrower should have experience with the type of real estate being purchased. Rapidly appreciating cryptocurrency can dramatically increase the net worth of the investor, allowing her to qualify for a loan based on the value of her crypto. The liquidity and the experience must be addressed with other approaches, but the net worth can be substantially improved using the value of cryptocurrency.

Cryptocurrency and Equity

When it comes to addressing equity instead of debt, the uses of cryptocurrency are different. In the most naïve case, you can just buy the property with cryptocurrency (if the seller owns it free and clear—no debt). But don't think of this as using currency to purchase equity. Both the real estate and the cryptocurrency are assets that are owned. And for both of them the value of the asset minus any debt represents equity in the asset. Instead of purchasing real estate with cryptocurrency, you are trading your equity in the cryptocurrency for equity in the real estate. The seller is not selling the property but trading his equity in the real estate for equity in cryptocurrency. At first glance, this may seem like a more complex way of looking at the transaction, but when you view the transaction this way it is much easier to really understand the opportunities to create alternative deal structures.

Thinking of the transaction as an exchange of equities now opens up all the possible things the equity can be traded for. It also raises the idea that the equity can be traded for a combination of other assets. For example, the equity can be traded for part fiat currency and part cryptocurrency. It could be traded for another piece of real estate plus a note (which would be an asset to the seller and a liability to the buyer) plus cryptocurrency. Essentially, any combination of assets could be used to satisfy the seller's investment objectives. When you apply these techniques, the conversation isn't about price of the property. Price is really an artificial construct anyway. Price is only used because of the convention to denominate all equities in fiat currency. Any savvy investor should be looking at income, appreciation, tax advantages—the overall return on their equity, and not price.

Consider this unrelated example to drive home the point: I have an apple and you have an orange. If I would prefer an orange and you would prefer an apple, we would likely trade. If we traded, would I have a capital gain? Would you? No one knows. At least, no one knows unless I put a price on the apple of $1 and you put a price on the orange of $1.50. With those prices on the fruit, it appears that the orange is 'objectively' valued at 50% more than the apple. We might still trade, but won't that exchange be more problematic for you? The psychological effect of the difference in price could kill the exchange, even if the apple is worth more to you than the orange.

Real estate and cryptocurrency are even less amenable to pricing than the apple and the orange. The acceptable price of cryptocurrency could be very different for different investors depending on their risk tolerance, the volatility of the cryptocurrency, and the role of the cryptocurrency in the assets of the investor (how much of their net worth is represented by the cryptocurrency). A seller with no exposure to the highly appreciating world of cryptocurrency may value receiving cryptocurrency for at least some of their equity. A buyer with a substantial stake in the cryptocurrency may value the stability of the real estate or its income potential as a risk mitigation measure for their cryptocurrency. In this case, an exchange greatly benefits both parties.

With real estate deals, there are some common breakpoints in the debt/equity stack that often make sense to use cryptocurrency. On the buyer's side, the capital stack often is comprised of a senior debt and a down payment. The amount of the down payment could be cryptocurrency. There is a similar breakpoint in the seller's capital stack (this usually consists of loans and equity). It is usually not possible for the seller to get the lender to accept cryptocurrency as repayment of the loan (at least not yet). So it is the difference between the loan payoff and the purchase price (adjusted by any closing costs) that would be in the seller's control to exchange for cryptocurrency. This amount could be further reduced by the presence of partners. It may be that the general partner seller can only exchange her own equity for cryptocurrency; partners may not be as sophisticated or may have different investment objectives. And it may not be desirable for a seller to trade all their equity for cryptocurrency. The seller may need fiat for another project or may want to diversify into multiple types of assets.

With any asset exchange, but especially with crypto since it is so volatile and is such a new type of asset, there may be a desire for some sort of guarantee or failsafe in order to make the exchange. A common approach with real estate, for example, is for the seller to rent the property or guarantee rent on the property for some amount of time. Another, less used approach, is the buyback. A property seller can offer to buy back the property after a certain amount of time for a previously agreed upon price. This approach is sometimes used when a seller needs a temporary break from a property or wants to change the property's use before buying it back. But the approach is also used to mitigate the buyer's risk; if everything goes south the seller will buy it back in three years.

A similar guarantee can be used for cryptocurrency. The person trading the cryptocurrency for real estate can offer to buy the crypto back after an agreed amount of time and at an agreed value (usually the same value placed on it for the original exchange). This eliminates the seller's concerns that the cryptocurrency will become worthless while preserving the ability to make substantial gains with the crypto. These types of guarantees may be necessary to close deals, especially early in the game of exchanging real estate for crypto.

Techniques for Leasehold Control

When the desired control of the real estate is a leasehold (you are renting the real estate), the dynamics of the deal and applicability of cryptocurrency changes. Since ownership is not being transferred, there is no need to address debt or equity. Instead, we have the security deposit and the rent. Either of these may be structured to include cryptocurrency.

A security deposit is provided to the real estate owner to cover damages to the property during the lease and provide additional skin in the game for the renter. Using cryptocurrency as the security deposit could be attractive to a landlord, since it has the potential of increasing in value, thus providing additional security over time. It might be necessary, however, to provide additional crypto if the value of the cryptocurrency drops.

Paying rent with cryptocurrency is also possible, but there are some additional considerations that must be addressed. Over the course of the lease, the value of the cryptocurrency will certainly vary. Deciding how much crypto to provide for each rent payment may be structured one of two ways. One approach is to provide a fixed quantity of crypto (say 100 TROPTIONS per month). This approach works like dollar-cost averaging in buying stocks. Over time the landlord will get an average price for the cryptocurrency. For rapidly appreciating crypto, this approach works to the considerable advantage of the landlord.

The other approach is to provide a fixed dollar amount of the cryptocurrency with each rent payment. You and the landlord should identify an independent third party or site that can determine the value of the cryptocurrency at any particular time. There are several websites that provide values for various cryptocurrencies. One of these is https://xchain.io. On this site you can search for a cryptocurrency and find its estimated current price. You would determine a new price and a new amount of cryptocurrency monthly based on the site's price and pay that amount. This approach attempts to provide the same fiat equivalent value each month rather than the same number of tokens of cryptocurrency.

As with structuring a purchase, the rent can be provided partially in cash and partially in other assets like cryptocurrency. It is not necessary for rent to be all fiat or all crypto. In fact, crypto might be used as a sweetener over a basic rent to compete against other potential tenants. Or perhaps sufficient fiat currency rent might be used to cover the landlord's property expenses and additional rent paid in crypto (this is similar in a purchase to paying the seller's loan with cash and his equity with crypto).

Techniques for Option Control

Another approach to control of real estate is to use an option. This is usually an option to buy and may be combined with a lease as a lease option. An option is usually a nominal payment that ties up the property so that a potential buyer can explore the feasibility of the property for their purposes. When developing the property requires rezoning or other approvals that can take months or even years to complete, an option is the preferred approach.

Cryptocurrency can be used as the option payment. The property owner gets an asset that may appreciate, and the buyer may be able to obtain the option with an asset that has already appreciated so that his basis in the asset is much less than the option price.

Often the option payment is credited toward the down payment. Using cryptocurrency as the option payment may also be a step toward using crypto in the ultimate sale.

Cryptocurrency and Transaction Fees

There are numerous transaction costs associated with a real estate sale. Most of those costs are to third parties that are operating as businesses and are unlikely to accept cryptocurrency for payment. But as crypto becomes more common and more accepted in normal transactions, these businesses may start to accept crypto for transaction fees.

But there are several common participants in real estate deals that have incentives to accept cryptocurrency for payment. The first is the real estate broker. I have been involved in transactions where the brokers agreed to accept cryptocurrency for part of their commission. Brokers are paid at closing, and do not receive a commission unless a sale (or lease) closes. Brokers then have considerable incentive to ensure a deal closes and can exercise flexibility as long as they receive adequate compensation. When the option is a lost sale and no commission at all, cryptocurrency is a significant improvement. Further, if the seller is accepting crypto-currency as part of the deal, it may not be feasible for the seller to provide fiat to a broker. The broker commission could kill the deal. In these cases, the broker is strongly incentivized to accept crypto-currency as all or part of her commission.

A second transaction participant is the wholesaler. A wholesaler gets a property under contract and sells his interest in the contract to a third party. The wholesaler has little to no money in the contract (maybe a deposit), and a profit in an appreciating asset can be an attractive wholesale fee. Most wholesalers intend to combine their fees to use them in other real estate deals that will build a portfolio of assets. A cryptocurrency that can be used to structure real estate deals is just as good as fiat currency in that situation.

A third transaction fee is the deposit, also known as the earnest money. How this is paid is the seller's decision. I have used crypto-currency as deposit in several transactions. The crypto can buy time to raise additional fiat if necessary for the deal. Usually a deposit is refundable until the end of the due diligence period in a contract. This fact makes it less of a seller risk to allow the deposit to be cryptocurrency, even if it must later be replaced with fiat currency before it 'goes hard'—becomes nonrefundable. There are several purposes for a deposit. The first is to put 'skin in the game' for the buyer. It demonstrates the buyer's seriousness to complete the transaction. Another main purpose is to provide compensation to the seller for the lost time when the buyer takes the property off market. The deposit acts as liquidated damages. And lastly, a deposit demonstrates an exchange of value that is necessary to make a contract valid. Cryptocurrency is actually quite a good choice to support all of these purposes.

Summary

In any particular deal there are multiple opportunities to use cryptocurrency. Crypto can be used to facilitate the debt. Crypto can be used to trade the seller for all or part of his equity. And crypto can be used to pay transaction fees. A smart investor might use cryptocurrency in more than one way in any particular deal. But any ability to use cryptocurrency may give the investor a competitive advantage over other investors who can't. A crypto savvy investor can do a variety of deals that she couldn't do before. And an investor who can tap into the value of cryptocurrency opens up new investor and real estate markets that did not exist before.

CHAPTER SEVEN

CRYPTOCURRENCY – REAL ESTATE SALE MECHANICS

I N THE PREVIOUS FEW chapters, I discussed how to structure real estate sales incorporating cryptocurrency. These structures are good high-level overviews, but, as they say, the devil is in the details. Any real estate transaction is complex. Anyone who has been to a real estate closing and had their hand cramp from the number of signatures required on the (usually hundreds of pages of) documents knows exactly what I mean. Cryptocurrency is new, and crypto real estate transactions are few. Most of the professionals usually involved in real estate transactions have no idea how to incorporate cryptocurrency. Even worse, many of the professionals involved are in extremely risk-averse professions (lawyers, title companies, lenders). Many are unwilling even to consider a cryptocurrency transaction if they can't find someone willing to tell them authoritatively how to do it and be liable for that process besides them.

As cryptocurrency transactions become more prevalent, these issues will disappear. But for those of us who are blazing a trail of using cryptocurrency for real estate transactions—and perhaps defining how these transactions can get done—we have to become the experts and learn to guide the professionals through the process. The challenges faced in completing crypto transactions were often a surprise to me. It took persistence, collaboration, and more than a little creativity to get transactions closed. The tactics described in this chapter are based on real-world transactions and not just theory.

There is one particular attribute of cryptocurrency transactions that plays a particularly important role in closing a real estate deal. That is the immutability of the transaction. If a mistake is made with any other real estate transaction, the paperwork can be modified and re-signed. Once cryptocurrency is sent from one wallet to another, no third party can get it back. Only the recipient can decide to return it. The permanence of the transaction has important implications for the order of closing and for the comfort of closing attorneys in handling the transactions. There are best practices to eliminating these risks and smoothing the transaction process that have worked in previous transactions.

Providers and their Roles in a Cryptocurrency Transaction

It takes a team to invest in real estate. The team includes brokers and lenders, title attorneys, managers, investors, sellers, buyers, securities attorneys, insurance companies, escrow agents, and often others with expertise specific to a deal. Many of these people have to do their jobs somewhat differently when cryptocurrency is involved. And it isn't obvious from the outside just what those difference are going to be. Cryptocurrency is also a rapidly changing and evolving landscape. What wasn't possible a couple of years ago may be possible today and routine next year.

Title/Closing Companies

The person or company that closes a real estate sale is different in different states. In some it is a title company. In others it is an attorney. Regardless of who pulls all the paperwork together and runs the closing, they end up doing the same job. They assemble all the paperwork and make sure the money and title move to the right places. When crypto is involved, the process for moving it is different than for fiat currency. Fiat is transferred by wires or cashier's checks. The actual recipients are banks (on behalf of the parties to the transaction) and bank accounts. The timing of wires and the methods of transfer are well honed—even if it always seems like something breaks during a closing. But cryptocurrency opens an alternative channel for the flow of the currency. Crypto is transferred directly from a wallet to a wallet, likely owned by the buyer and seller, respectively. It is possible for the crypto to be held by a third-party trustee, and industries are emerging to provide just that service. But most of the title companies I have talked with do not want to touch cryptocurrency themselves, mainly because they just don't know how to do it and are afraid of screwing it up.

If a title attorney won't assist with the transfer of the cryptocurrency, then the order of closing has to be adapted so that the transfer can happen at the appropriate time, be confirmed, and the rest of closing completed. I will describe the particular order of closing I used in my first transaction later in this chapter.

As companies like Prime Trust (https://primetrust.com) have emerged to handle cryptocurrency escrows and hold crypto in accounts much like bank accounts, they are becoming a better choice for a trusted third party. But be careful. Even the most forward-looking companies agree to handle only a handful of the most popular cryptocurrencies. Chances are that the cryptocurrency you want to trade or exchange will not be on the exclusive list. A big push for decentralized exchanges that can handle any cryptocurrency is occurring in the industry, but it will take time until all the mechanisms are in place. Until then, you will likely be limited to direct buyer to seller exchanges or convincing a third party to hold the crypto in a wallet and distributing it based on instructions, just as escrow companies are supposed to do.

Title Insurance

Title insurance companies are among the most risk averse in the world. In 2017 when I did my first crypto deal in real estate, no title insurance company would insure the title at closing. There really is no good reason for their reluctance. A deed is still a deed. It's exactly the same deed we would have obtained if the sale was for cash. And the previous owners of the property are exactly the same previous owners there would have been if the property was sold for cash. There is no difference in the risk involved with this transaction versus any other. But nevertheless, title companies refused to consider issuing title because cryptocurrency was involved in the transaction—at least at closing.

The day after closing, however, when I owned the property, there was no impediment to obtaining title insurance for a property I owned. It was a simple matter to obtain the title insurance then. Does it matter if you have to go 24 hours without title insurance? I suspect the odds are astronomical that something that didn't come up in a title search would somehow emerge during that timeframe. But be prepared to understand and accept that risk if you wait a day to get title insurance.

While it may make no difference to you, if you have a lender, they may not be willing to proceed to closing unless they can get title insurance at closing. And their reluctance may prevent the deal from happening. Fortunately, we are no longer in 2017. There are a few title companies that are not so freaked out about cryptocurrency, and once one or two of them complete a few transactions, the power of competition will turn this from an impossible problem to an easy fix. As I write this, title insurance may be challenging but not impossible, and in one or two years it will be easy.

Escrow Agents

It is common for the earnest money deposit and other monies involved in the transaction to be held in bank accounts by escrow agents (who are often the same title companies or real estate attorneys who do the closings). There is no reason this cannot be done the same way with cryptocurrency. The crypto would be held in a wallet owned by the escrow company. You would send the crypto to their wallet. At closing or at other times depending on the contract, the escrow agent could send the crypto to the appropriate party. It's actually much easier than fiat currency in a bank.

But having and maintaining a wallet for the cryptocurrency is unfamiliar to most escrow agents. And the idea that if they lose their pass phrase to the account that the account would be lost is, not unreasonably, frightening. These attorneys of course have usernames and passwords to log in to online banking for their fiat accounts. Crypto is similar to online banking in that way but with the exception that if you lose your username or password, you can call the bank, prove your identity, and reset it. Someone else (the bank) is actually fundamentally responsible for holding the money, not the escrow agent.

Again, the advent of crypto escrow agents alleviates this fear. They act just like the bank for current fiat currencies. But as I pointed out, their ability to hold crypto is rudimentary and focused solely on a few coins and tokens. It may be necessary to find a third party who is not a usual escrow agent or agree that one or the other of the buyer and seller would be trustworthy enough to hold the crypto until the larger infrastructure is in place.

Lenders/Mortgage Brokers

When real estate is purchased with a mortgage, the lender has a say in all aspects of the deal. They will make requirements and conditions that reduce their risk. I have spoken with numerous lenders over the past few years on multiple projects. Most of the discussion has been around projects where cryptocurrency was all or part of the down payment. Here are the questions that I am asked the most and the sometimes multifaceted answers that are required:

- **How do I know what the value of the cryptocurrency is?** The simplest answer to this, of course, is to give them a website where they can look up the price of the cryptocurrency. But I have rarely found that to be sufficient. There is an underlying concern here that the cryptocurrency is actually worthless and is being used to prop up the price of the asset to get a bigger loan. This concern you would think would be addressed by getting a formal third party appraisal from a reputable company. But even an appraisal that supports the purchase price does not always answer this question. If you get to that point and the lender still balks, find another lender.

- **Why don't you just sell it and use cash?** This financial advice from someone who obviously knows nothing about cryptocurrency is partially an attempt to get an answer about the liquidity of the cryptocurrency and partially just an attempt to make life easier for the lender. The liquidity aspect is somewhat relevant to the deal and gets to the heart of whether the crypto is really an asset. But the only one who really needs to be concerned about the liquidity of the crypto is the one receiving it; the seller. If the liquidity is sufficient for them, why should the lender care? Whether the crypto is liquid or not, the right answer to this question is that the sale of the cryptocurrency has tax consequences that cannot be managed as easily as when the cryptocurrency is part of the deal. This is the truth and is a really good reason to exchange crypto for real estate rather than cashing it in first. At this point, though, I have to mention that most of the touted sales of real estate for Bitcoin have been just such sales—they sold the Bitcoin to get cash to buy the real estate. They were not really Bitcoin for real estate.

- **What if the crypto price changes between now and closing? Will you still be able to close?** These questions raise a valid concern about the volatility of the cryptocurrency. The answer to this question, however, depends on how the cryptocurrency portion of the exchange is handled in the contract. I will go into more details about options for the crypto price in the contract later in this chapter. What I typically propose is that the crypto price be checked on the reference site at 5:00 pm on the day prior to closing and that price be used to value the crypto on the day of closing. This approach puts the volatility risk prior to closing on the buyer and after closing on the seller. As long as the transaction does not require all of my cryptocurrency, there is sufficient contingency to cover closing, even if the price drops between now and then.

It is worth your while to have your answers to these questions ready when you speak with a lender. They will ask these questions, and it helps if you have thought it through from the lender's perspective.

With all that said, as it stands right now in 2021, you might as well forget about working with banks or any other highly regulated lenders if you have cryptocurrency as part of the transaction and you don't plan to liquidate it to actually provide cash at closing. As much as any particular bankers would like to accept cryptocurrency, the banking regulations just have not caught up with the idea of crypto as an asset. A banker would be taking a risk in underwriting the project, and very few bankers will take that risk. You should plan on working with less regulated lenders like private lenders—just as you would with any transaction that is a little out of the ordinary.

There is one approach, however, that can please even the stodgiest lender, but it requires flexibility on both your part and your seller's. You can buy into the equity of the property with the cryptocurrency so that for a short time you and the seller are partners in the property. Then instead of a purchase money loan, you get a refinance. The funds from the refinance take the place of the purchase mortgage you would have obtained, and the seller's ownership interest is bought with the refinance money. This is referred to as a leveraged buyout, and it works well as a way of reducing the lender reluctance to accept cryptocurrency as part of the deal. By the time the refinance is taking place, there is no cryptocurrency in the project, only equity.

Real Estate Brokers

Real estate brokers and agents are integral to the sale or lease of real property. They are often the ones who bring buyers and sellers together and usually participate in the negotiations for the sale.

Brokers also help smooth the purchase process, following up with other providers and ensuring that everything continues to move forward. A broker who understands cryptocurrency has another set of tools to make a deal and a larger market of buyers. A broker who doesn't understand cryptocurrency can completely kill a cryptocurrency for real estate approach and prevent the seller from selling their property. An informed broker can help ensure all the other providers understand the nuances of using cryptocurrency and make the connections necessary to fill any gaps in expertise or services.

Real estate brokers are typically paid a commission in cash at closing, and that is their primary source of income. Creative brokers have always found alternative ways to be paid when the sales don't include cash. Sometimes they take a note and get paid over time. Sometimes they accept a piece of property or equity in the real estate being purchased. A question every real estate broker should ask is whether they will accept cryptocurrency as all or part of their commission—especially if the rest of the deal does not include fiat currency as part of the transaction. If they won't—or can't—accept cryptocurrency, they may be the reason a deal can't close if there isn't sufficient cash to satisfy the commission.

Next Generation Providers

As cryptocurrency develops and expands, alternative providers are developing capabilities that fill many of these roles, but with crypto expertise as part of their offerings. There are already real estate brokers and agents who understand how to incorporate cryptocurrency into a deal and how to negotiate with a seller to accept it (I'm one, but there are others). Companies are already chartered who can hold cryptocurrency in escrow. And there are lenders who are lending against cryptocurrency.

But there are also new capabilities that leverage other cryptocurrency approaches to work within real estate. There are companies (https://propy.com, for example) that provide capability for online real estate offers and work through the entire sales process from offer through contract to closing. For many of their closings, they liquidate the cryptocurrency and move cash from buyer to seller, but they do provide an online infrastructure for real estate deals that includes cryptocurrency.

Another company, ShelterZoom, which has launched a new product called DocuWalk (https://docuwalk.com), aims to provide an online capability for making offers, negotiating contracts, and contract execution. They use smart contracts and support online collaboration and negotiation among multiple parties.

As we will see in later chapters, some of these capabilities use other aspects of blockchain technology and cryptocurrency. But they aim to provide a more modern, seamless approach to real estate transactions. And being born of cryptocurrency technologies, they are naturally friendly to crypto transactions.

Real Estate Contract Options for Cryptocurrency

When putting together an offer of cryptocurrency for real estate, you have to include some specifics about how the cryptocurrency is treated in the contract. Most important is defining the quantity of cryptocurrency being offered. When you specify a purchase price in most contracts, the price is in U.S. dollars and the number of dollars is specified. If the dollars devalue between contract and closing, it is nevertheless understood that the same number of dollars is provided at closing.

Since cryptocurrency is really an asset that has an intrinsic number of units as well as an ever-changing value in fiat currency, you really must specify what cryptocurrency is being provided either in value or in units. For example, suppose you are offering $1,000,000 on an apartment complex where you intend to get a $600,000 dollar loan secured by the property and provide $400,000 worth of cryptocurrency. There are really two alternatives for specifying the amount of cryptocurrency. Below are examples of formal contract language for each of the options similar to what I have used in previous transactions:

- Example 1: At the Closing, Buyer shall deliver to Seller an amount of XTROPTIONS.GOLD cryptocurrency equal in value to Four Hundred Thousand Dollars ($400,000.00) (the "Crypto"), as determined by the price shown on the https://xchain.io website at 5:00 pm on the day prior to closing.
- Example 2: At the Closing, Buyer shall deliver to Seller Ninety-One Thousand, Five Hundred and Thirty-Three Point One Eight Zero Eight (91,533.1808) XTROPTIONS.GOLD.

In the first example, we specify a dollar value for the cryptocurrency, in this case $400,000. We also specify the exact cryptocurrency token (or coin) that is being transferred. It is not sufficient to say cryptocurrency. After all, different cryptocurrencies are like different assets or even different types of fiat. They have varying values, desirability, and liquidity. Imagine in a normal real estate contract if you expected to receive one million dollars and instead got one million Venezuelan Bolivars. Specifying the actual currency being delivered is important in all contracts, including those that include cryptocurrency.

In the first example, we must also determine how and when we will value the cryptocurrency. Since XTROPTIONS.GOLD is the cryptocurrency in the example, we use https://xchain.io as the website where we obtain its independently determined price. Different cryptocurrencies will require different sites or approaches for determining value. Very popular crypto like Bitcoin may have several alternatives for assessing price (those prices should be similar but not exact at different sites at the same time). Until there is some central clearinghouse for all cryptocurrency prices—the closest today is https://coinmarketcap.com, but it does not include all cryptocurrencies—we should specify the reference site.

It is also important to specify when the token will be valued. The two most likely times are at the time of contract execution and at the time of contract closing. In the example we set the value at 5:00 pm on the day prior to closing, so we had some time to set all the numbers in the closing documents. We did not specify a time zone, but if buyer, seller, and property are not in the same time zone it should probably also be specified. Just this year, if we were using Bitcoin, which has been far more volatile than XTROPTIONS. GOLD this year, if our contract execution was on October 1, 2020 and our closing on December 1, 2020, the difference in value would be $10,907 (on October 1) and $19,151 (on December 1). That's quite a difference in the amount of Bitcoin that would be required for closing. On the $400,000 it would be 400,000/10,907=36.6736958 Bitcoin on October 1 and 400,000/19,151=20.8866378 Bitcoin on December 1. This is an extreme jump, but it does illustrate the potential issues.

When you specify a valuation time at contract execution, the seller is at risk from the time of contract execution until closing for any value changes in the cryptocurrency. In the above example, I think the seller would be glad to take the risk, since the price nearly doubled. If the price had decreased, the seller would be obliged to take less in dollar value for their property at closing. On the other hand, the seller can fix the dollar value of his property by valuing the cryptocurrency at closing instead. The buyer is then at risk for pricing changes between contract and closing.

The second example is much simpler. It merely states that a certain amount of cryptocurrency is being provided for the property. In this case, you would likely specify the total price as $600,000 plus 91,533.1808 XTROPTIONS.GOLD. In that example I based the number of XTROPTIONS.GOLD on an estimated price of $4.37 per token. The number of tokens is specified to four decimal places. Typically, cryptocurrency can be specified up to eight decimal places (with Bitcoin, the eighth decimal place is called the Satoshi). For cryptocurrencies that trade at less than or even near $1.00, it may seem like overkill to specify so many digits. But if the cryptocurrency increases in value like Bitcoin to the point where one coin is worth tens of thousands or even hundreds of thousands of dollars, those decimal places could become significant.

You will note there is no relation to fiat currency of any type in the specification in example 2. In this case, the sale is not denominated solely in fiat. It is fiat plus assets. The buyer and seller should come to an agreement on how to value the asset being exchanged, if only so that their tax filings will agree. But that value is undetermined by anything external to the deal. Below is another example from a contract about valuing the cryptocurrency in a transaction that makes this indeterminacy more explicit.

- **WHEREAS,** Buyer owns a Cryptocurrency described as "XTROPTIONS.GOLD" and wishes to pay a portion of purchase consideration for the LLC and its real property in form of this Cryptocurrency.

- **WHEREAS,** Buyer and Seller acknowledge that it is difficult to value the Cryptocurrency due in part to a lack of tangible value presently and have agreed to value this transaction/ sale price at Cash and or Seller Note at face value plus the XTROPTIONS.GOLD consideration with the XTROPTIONS.

GOLD mutually valued at $10,000, as full consideration for this sale and purchase of LLC and its related real property. It is agreed that the Buyer and Seller have agreed to determine the "cash value" of these XTROPTIONS.GOLD to be $10,000 for their purpose of establishing sale and purchase basis as further set forth in section X.X of this agreement. . .

Consideration. The Purchase Price shall be paid by Buyer as follows:

a. Within three (3) business days after the date of receipt by Buyer of a fully executed copy of this Agreement (the "Effective Date"), Buyer shall deposit into a separate cryptocurrency wallet with wallet access information provided to _____ (the "Escrow Agent") the sum of Ten Thousand (10,000.00) XTROPTIONS.GOLD, a cryptocurrency (the "Deposit"). The Deposit shall be held in that separate electronic wallet until distributed as later specified in this contract.

b. The balance of the Purchase Price, subject to adjustments and apportionments as set forth herein, shall be paid by Buyer at Closing, of which $600,000 shall be in a seller note secured by the property (the "Note") and 90,000 of XTROPTIONS.GOLD, provided via electronic transfer to a Seller wallet, at which time the Deposit shall be credited against the Purchase Price and also transferred to the Seller wallet.

In this example, the buyer and seller explicitly value the remaining property equity and the XTROPTIONS.GOLD being exchanged at a value of $10,000. All the other numbers in the deal remain the same as the earlier examples. The note is in the amount of

$600,000. If the purchase price were $1,000,000, the remaining $400,000 would mean XTROPTIONS.GOLD were valued at $4/token. How does this square with a jointly estimated value of $10,000? Is this reasonable? The answer, as with most valuation questions is, "it depends". If the seller reasonably believes that the XTROPTIONS. GOLD could become worthless and is taking a risk that the value will be something more, a $10,000 valuation could make sense. We have to ask also whether the $1,000,000 original value of the apartment complex was reasonable. Perhaps the buyer is substantially overpaying because of the seller's flexibility in terms and the apartment complex is really only worth $600,000. If a formal appraisal is performed as part of the sale, I think you would expect that the buyer and seller would set the value of the XTROPTIONS.GOLD to be the difference between the appraised value (or a value near it) and the dollar value of the note.

The point that should be emphasized here is that value (of real estate and of cryptocurrency) is not a fixed number but can change based on the deal terms, the other considerations of the sale, the proposed use of the property, and numerous other factors. By constructing the price in the contract as asset for asset, you and the seller have full flexibility to mutually determine an appropriate value for each of your assets as long as the exchange balances.

There is another option for cryptocurrency specification that is worth exploring here. When the buyer has cryptocurrency that has greatly appreciated, much of the value of the cryptocurrency would be taxed as capital gains when it is exchanged for real estate. Similarly, if the seller of the real estate has owned the property for a long time, much of the value of the property may also be subject to capital gains tax. In this case, both parties would be hit with substantial capital gains taxes even though no fiat currency exchanges hands (there is no cash to pay the taxes). An alternative is to create a note denominated in cryptocurrency, secured by cryptocurrency, and paid by cryptocurrency. The capital gains taxes are still due when the cryptocurrency is received by the seller, but by creating a note, that portion of the sale becomes an installment sale and taxes would only be due on the part of the cryptocurrency for which the seller has "constructive receipt". I have proposed transactions that include this approach, but I have not yet closed one. As always, you must consult your legal and accounting professionals to ensure that your approach to a transaction falls within the legal and tax regulations and rulings in force at the time.

Tax Treatment for Real Estate/Crypto Exchanges

As I am not an accountant, I approach the topic of tax treatment for crypto to real estate exchanges with some trepidation, but I have spoken with several accountants and heard from additional investors who have passed along what their accountants have said. Some of these opinions disagree. Also, the landscape is rapidly changing. Anything I say now may be obsolete in six months, never mind five years. Please take everything here as food for thought and possible ways of looking at the tax advantages and consequences of cryptocurrency for real estate deals. Before you make an investment decision, consult a competent professional yourself. Lastly, I will only be discussing U.S. tax implications. I imagine many countries will follow similar treatment, but you should check. With all these caveats in mind, let's plunge in.

Most cryptocurrencies (note I said most, not all; there are exceptions) are considered to be assets that can be owned, traded, and sold. In the U.S., the Internal Revenue Service (IRS) expects someone acquiring an asset to set a basis (the purchase price adjusted by any other costs or benefits). When the asset is sold or exchanged, the IRS wants you to set the basis of what you have gotten in exchange (that's easy when it's fiat currency but more challenging when you get something else). The difference between the new basis in the new asset and the basis you had at acquisition is your capital gain.

If you held the cryptocurrency for less than a year, the capital gain is known as short-term. If you held it for longer than a year it is called long-term. The tax treatments are different. Short-term capital gains are generally taxed like ordinary income at your normal tax rate for the top end of your income. Long-term capital gains are generally capped at 20% right now. But all of these values can change based on your other income and expenses.

Since cryptocurrency is famous for its ability to appreciate, most cryptocurrency investors will have to deal with substantial capital gains when they sell or exchange the cryptocurrency. Yes, it hurts. Writing a big check to the IRS if you sell crypto will be a painful experience. But it only happens because you made a killing, so don't feel too bad. Enjoy the win. And pay your taxes. In 2017 the IRS had no real capability to find you. After all, the only record is an impenetrable wallet address, not your name and contact info. But in 2021, most of the exchanges perform KYC and AML checks. They have your contact info. And the IRS won a lawsuit for one primary exchange to provide the contact and banking info of its users who made more than $10,000 on cryptocurrency. In 2020, for the first time, there will be a checkbox on the tax forms asking if you bought, sold, exchanged, or traded any cryptocurrency this year. Not checking that box will come back to bite you if you are investing in cryptocurrency. Again, enjoy the win. Pay your taxes.

The real difficulty comes in when you buy real estate with cryptocurrency. It is possible for both you and the seller of the real estate to have substantial capital gains and no cash anywhere in the deal to pay it. That lack of cash will kill the deal. This is the situation where structuring the deal properly can defer, delay, or reduce the tax.

I have heard from at least one accountant that a properly structured asset for asset exchange—where neither asset is denominated or valued in fiat currency—does not have a tax consequence. I present that point of view for thoroughness. My accountant does not agree, and I follow my accountant's advice. I welcome comments from readers who have studied the issue and can provide a professional opinion that differs.

For exchanges where neither the crypto nor the real estate are denominated in dollars, what is the value of each property? While saying that there is no tax consequence is probably not the answer, there is a wide range of possible values that could be agreed upon by a willing buyer and seller. The deal will have competing objectives. If the seller (or buyer) wants or needs to have a certain return on their investment, there may be reasons to increase the notional sale price. If capital gain is the primary issue, there may be reasons to have a low or negligible sale price. When real estate (or cryptocurrency) is purchased directly with fiat currency, there is no price flexibility. The fiat currency is the denomination of value. A dollar is worth a dollar. One advantage of direct exchange is the flexibility to set the price at a point that is advantageous to the buyer and seller.

One of the principal advantages of investing in real estate is the use of the 1031 tax deferred exchange. When you sell one investment property and invest in a 'like' property (in the case of investment real estate, any other investment real estate is considered to be 'like'), it is possible to defer the capital gains on the sale of the original property. There are many rules about how the exchange has to be done, including strict timelines and a requirement to purchase a larger property with more debt. I won't go into all the details of a 1031 exchange here; many books cover it in detail. The point is that you get to reinvest all the proceeds of the sale without taking a 20% hit. That allows you to buy a bigger property and grow your wealth faster.

When cryptocurrency is involved, you are generally not able to implement a 1031 exchange. Cryptocurrency and real estate are not 'like' investments, so trading property for crypto will not be eligible for tax deferral using 1031. As of January 1, 2018, the IRS says that exchanging one cryptocurrency for another is also not a like kind exchange. The simplest thing to do is forget about like kind exchanges when using cryptocurrency. This may change, so if it would help you to do a 1031 exchange when using cryptocurrency check with your accounting professional and get up-to-date advice.

One intriguing possibility is to treat the cryptocurrency the same way you do cash in a 1031 exchange. You send the crypto to a qualified intermediary at closing who holds it. If you follow the same timing rules as for a cash purchase and use the cryptocurrency in a real estate deal that meets the 1031 exchange criteria, would you be able to similarly qualify for tax deferral? I believe this approach would work, but I don't know anyone who has tried it. Since cryptocurrency for real estate transactions are more challenging than cash transactions, you would likely want the replacement property identified before you closed on the initial property.

Another way of managing capital gains when exchanging cryptocurrency for real estate is to use an installment sale. For most real estate deals, an installment sale is accomplished by using seller financing. The seller is paid their principal over time and owes capital gains on the principal they receive. The gain does not go away, but acknowledging the gain in smaller chunks makes it easier to manage over time. If the cryptocurrency is paid over time, the capital gain from the cryptocurrency (for the buyer) and the real estate (for the seller) can both be treated as installment sales. The details of the exchange over time are important. The gain is due when the seller has constructive receipt of the asset. Below is an example of a contract clause that would create an installment sale using the earlier example of a $1,000,000 property being sold for $600,000 plus $400,000 in cryptocurrency.

- At the Closing, Buyer shall deliver to Seller a non-recourse promissory note (in the form attached hereto as Exhibit "C") (the "Note") for an amount of XTROPTIONS.GOLD, a cryptocurrency equal in value to Four Hundred Thousand Dollars ($400,000.00), less the amount of the Deposit which shall be credited against the Note, as determined by the price shown on the https://troptionsexchange.com website at 5:00 pm on the day prior to closing. The Note shall be secured by a pledge and security agreement whereby Buyer pledges an equivalent amount of XTROPTIONS.GOLD.

Note that in this case I changed the website for valuing XTROPTIONS.GOLD. Also note that there is a separate attached promissory note and a pledge and security agreement. All these together implement, in essence, a note that is paid by cryptocurrency and secured by cryptocurrency. The full documents, suitably modified to remove buyer and seller information, may be available in my cryptocurrency and real estate members area. (You can sign up for membership at https://CryptoREBook.com).

Managing taxes is a challenging endeavor. The rules change constantly. The U.S. tax code is over 70,000 pages. No one knows all of it. But there are many accountants across the U.S. who specialize in tax treatment of real estate. No doubt over the next few years some accountants will specialize in cryptocurrency. The best advice I can give is to document your transactions, calculate your basis on each one, and be able to provide that information to your accountant. Pay your taxes.

Closing Process for Cryptocurrency

Very few title companies have closed sales where cryptocurrency plays a part. Most cryptocurrency for real estate sales are completed by liquidating the cryptocurrency and providing the resulting cash to the seller. As I've discussed in this chapter and earlier, there are substantial advantages that can be obtained by trading the cryptocurrency directly for the real estate. Having actually closed real estate for cryptocurrency transactions, I'm in a unique position to explain how the closing process differs from a standard closing.

Title companies or closing attorneys generally do not have the expertise or the processes in place to handle cryptocurrency. The ones I have worked with would rather not be the ones transferring crypto from one wallet to another, and they also would rather not hold cryptocurrency for any length of time. They have concerns about hacking, about losing the passwords, about mistaking the wallet addresses. These are legitimate concerns, but they are really the same concerns that we all have with money and accounts. There is one key difference, however. Once you transfer cryptocurrency from one wallet to another, there is no way (except the recipient transferring it back) to undo the transaction.

The immutability of the cryptocurrency transfer is the key issue in modifying the closing process for crypto transactions. You can't transfer the cryptocurrency until the critical elements of the rest of the process are also completed. I have found that the closing process in these transactions breaks into three sequential pieces.

The first step is to execute the closing agreements. These typically include the deed(s), any promissory notes and mortgages, the settlement statements, and any ancillary documents that are required in your particular jurisdiction. Some of these documents must be notarized and are typically executed in the presence of the settlement attorney. However, in the revised cryptocurrency process, these documents are held by the closing agent (settlement attorney or title company) in escrow and not recorded yet.

The second step is to transfer the cryptocurrency. Because all the other documents are executed, there is little risk that the real estate will not be transferred once the cryptocurrency is. The deed is already signed. In the closings I have participated in, I transferred the cryptocurrency to the seller's wallet myself. Note that to do the transfer will require a small amount of whatever cryptocurrency acts as a transfer fee for the particular cryptocurrency you are exchanging. For XTROPTIONS.GOLD, you would use Bitcoin. Transaction fees vary based on traffic but not based on the amount being transferred. It costs the same to transfer $1 billion in cryptocurrency as it costs to transfer $1 in crypto. Typical transaction fees are a few cents but in times of extremely high traffic, it can cost a few dollars. The speed of the transaction can also be selected (you can move the transaction up in priority by paying more), but I think the worst case is around $30–$50, and on most blockchains it is much less. (As an aside, notice how much cheaper this is than the standard wire fee at a bank and also notice that many fiat transfers cost a percentage of the amount being transferred. Cryptocurrency is far superior. It is faster, cheaper, more reliable, and eliminates many of the delays that can happen with wires.)

Verifying the transfer is actually much easier with cryptocurrency than with fiat. Since every transaction is public, anyone (you, the seller, the title company—anyone) can view the record of the cryptocurrency being moved from the buyer's wallet to the seller's wallet. All you have to know is one of the wallet addresses and which blockchain records the cryptocurrency. Verifying the transfer is something that a title company may be able to do independently if clear instructions are provided. The verification, likely in the form of a printout showing the link accessed, the date and time, and the transaction details, can be added to the closing documents and signed by all parties.

One safety measure that is often implemented to ensure accurate crypto transfer is to first do a trial transfer of a nominal amount of cryptocurrency. Sending, for example, a few dollars' worth of crypto proves that the addresses are correct and that the transfer approach works. The real transfer can usually be set up without having to re-enter the wallet addresses (the most likely source of error), reducing exposure to errors. Sending a trial amount is a best practice, really, for any large cryptocurrency transfer.

The third step is to record the relevant documents. These typically include the deed and any mortgages secured by real estate. This part of the process is identical to standard real estate closings.

The biggest change between the process described above and the standard real estate closing is the order of currency transfer. In a standard closing, all the funds are provided to the closing agent first using immediately available funds (wire transfers or cashier's checks). Then the closing documents are signed and recorded. Since the closing agent is not holding and dispersing the cryptocurrency, the closing documents have to be signed first (but withheld) and the cryptocurrency transferred afterwards.

What I have described above is a closing process that anyone can do using any title company. It takes the cryptocurrency-specific parts of the closing out of the hands of the title attorney and substitutes a verification document agreed upon between buyer and seller. However, as more transactions are done and more providers have experience with closing cryptocurrency transactions, this process will get easier. One service that will facilitate this process is the cryptocurrency escrow agent. If you use someone who knows how to hold and disperse cryptocurrency, the overall closing process can revert back to the traditional order, since the cryptocurrency can be verified as being held by a trusted third party. This service is available today. The most well-known provider is https://PrimeTrust.com. They provide all the escrow services necessary, but for a very limited number of cryptocurrencies.

Even more exciting are the opportunities to improve real estate closings using smart contracts. I will discuss these in more detail in a later chapter. But smart contracts are able to automatically transfer the cryptocurrency at the appropriate time as well as, potentially, record documents and disperse funds. A well-constructed smart contract could replace title attorneys (though one expects that it would be title attorneys creating and reviewing the smart contracts to ensure legal compliance; the closing agents don't go away, they just don't need to be there at execution of closing). As formal documents move to the blockchain in the form of smart contracts, property title and liens may also be, for all intents and purposes, cryptocurrency. It would then actually be easier for a smart contract to record title and mortgages than for title attorneys to do it.

There are a few companies that are already trying to set up closing processes entirely online using smart contracts. One of these is https://Propy.com. Propy lists and sells real estate where the seller is willing to accept cryptocurrency as part of the purchase price. They have an offer, contract, and closing process that operates online, though there are offline activities that have to happen (like recording title). Most of their closings liquidate the cryptocurrency and provide the cash to the seller rather than trade directly. But kudos to them for normalizing the process of offering on real estate with cryptocurrency and providing capability for the whole purchase process.

Another recent effort worth mentioning is from ShelterZoom. They have created a product called Docuways that has the ambition to be a one-stop shop for digital contracts. They have an easy-to-use collaboration platform that allows buyer and seller (and their representatives) to complete, negotiate, and sign contracts and other documents online. The templates would need to be created and imported to the sited, but all the contracts and closing documentation could be done online using their capability.

Well-designed smart contracts can actually automate the transfer of cryptocurrency. The transfer is automatically executed when other contract terms (for example, the execution of the deed) are satisfied. These contracts can make the transfer of cryptocurrency completely transparent and actually more certain and secure than fiat transfers.

As these capabilities and others roll out online, closings with cryptocurrency and real estate will become easier and more common. There are too many benefits from putting these documents on the blockchain to ignore. Today, however, it is necessary to implement work-arounds to ensure that smooth closings occur, even when the professionals involved are not crypto savvy.

Summary

Having alternative ways to construct deals is a competitive advantage for any real estate investor. Cryptocurrency provides a whole new set of tools for that toolbox. Crypto can help an investor obtain debt for an acquisition, and there are numerous ways for cryptocurrency to address a seller's equity as well. Smart investors can use cryptocurrency appreciation as a way of accelerating their wealth building and can dramatically increase their real estate portfolios.

The key to using cryptocurrency in real estate deals is to understand the principles of real estate exchange and apply those in structuring deals. Every deal should be viewed as exchanges of debt, equity, and control. When an investor frames their investments as exchanges, a wide variety of options emerge for trading her equity in cryptocurrency for equity in real estate (or vice versa).

Barter currencies like REXNET or TROPTIONS are ideal cryptocurrencies for use in real estate exchanges because their purpose is to be traded for other assets. Barter currencies will emerge as the principal crypto asset used in real estate investing. Learning how to use barter currencies now will give any investor an advantage as these currencies become better known and more widely used.

As with any new technology, cryptocurrency will have a learning curve. Those in the broader real estate industry, like brokers, title agents, and lenders, may need assistance for their first few cryptocurrency real estate deals. Investors should understand how crypto impacts real estate processes. They should be ready to answer questions and provide suggestions and resources for their teammates as they work to close these deals.

Over time—not necessarily a very long time given how quickly cryptocurrency is catching on—real estate deals involving cryptocurrency will become normal. By then, all investors will be doing them. For now, the investors who learn how to structure these deals will be the leaders who transform real estate deal-making with cryptocurrency.

SECTION III

TRANSFORMING OWNERSHIP

CHAPTER EIGHT

TOKENIZING REAL ESTATE

S ECURITY TOKEN OFFERINGS (STOs) are transforming how real estate is owned and how investors can participate.

Imagine that you are an investor with limited capital to invest. You would love to own a large apartment complex. You want to take advantage of all the economies of scale you get with such a property. You want higher quality properties with stable returns. You want what the investors with lots of capital want.

But you can't buy a property like that yourself. You could invest in a Real Estate Investment Trust (REIT), but you wouldn't be owning a property. You would be owning a portfolio of properties with the returns including both the good properties and the dogs. Your returns would be far less than with owning a good property.

If you are an accredited investor you could invest in a private placement offering (more about those later). If you are an unaccredited investor you may be able to invest in a private placement, also called a syndication, but you have to know someone. I mean that literally. You must have a preexisting relationship with the sponsor to be able to invest. That's a U.S. Securities and Exchange Commission (SEC) rule.

None of these options are open to most smaller investors (and I mean the size of their capital, not their heart or physical stature). There are good reasons for this; the SEC believes that people without much money may not know as much about how to invest it and tries to protect them from less regulated investments. But many private placements are less risky than REITS and provide bigger returns. If you've had training and understand what you are doing, it is just frustrating not being able to invest in these offerings.

Tokenization

Enter tokenization. With tokenization, small pieces of the property can be purchased and sold. These small pieces of ownership are implemented as cryptocurrency and called Security Token Offerings (STOs). The STO is a digital representation of partial ownership in a property. They can be bought and sold like cryptocurrency (with necessary restrictions that we will discuss later in this chapter). Property tokenization is the latest, and in my opinion best, way to allow smaller investors to own quality real estate. It is also an improved approach for the deal makers who generally use syndications to accomplish something similar.

Tokenization works for investors because they get improved liquidity, can invest smaller amounts, and can buy or sell a portion of their investment.

Tokenization works for sponsors (those who put together the deals) because they are easier to manage. The improved liquidity also benefits the sponsors who own part of the property themselves. And the reliance on smart contracts automates key functions like distributions and investor reports.

TICs, DSTs, and Syndications

To understand the benefits of tokenization, you must first understand the alternatives. What other ways do investors use to invest in a property? The main ones that I will discuss here are Tenant in Common (TIC) structures, Delaware Statutory Trusts (DST), and syndications.

TICs are often marketed as temporary places to put money that is subject to a 1031 exchange. There are many rules to completing a successful tax deferment under the 1031 section of the tax code. Among them are a requirement to identify replacement properties within 45 days and closing on the replacement property or properties within 180 days. TICs are often used as a failsafe to ensure a successful exchange if you can't find the property you really want. In a TIC, you own a fractional interest in the property directly. This makes it well suited to a 1031 exchange. In some of the other structures, you technically own membership interest in a limited liability company instead of directly in the real estate. You may not be able to do a 1031 exchange into those structures because you are trading interest in real estate for interest in a company (no longer like kind) even if the company is solely an owner of real estate.

Most TICs are large office buildings or other commercial buildings. The buildings are professionally managed, often by institutions who market them to investors who already own stocks or bonds in brokerage accounts associated with the institutions. Returns are usually good but not inspiring. If an investor wants to leave the investment, the manager will usually try to find a replacement investor, but there is no guarantee. Some of the larger institutions will guarantee to purchase an investor's position with their own funds until they can resell to a new investor.

TICs can be challenging to operate and maintain, since each investor in the TIC has full ownership of a fraction of the property.

Each investor has some decision-making authority, and each investor has to get their own financing if financing is used.

The Delaware Statutory Trust (DST) is an alternative to a TIC. With a DST, the investor is actually investing in a trust and holding fractional interest in the asset of the trust.

The DST provides limited liability to the investor, just as an LLC or a limited partnership does. But unlike a syndication (which we will discuss next), a 2004 IRS ruling allows DST ownership to qualify as a like kind for real estate 1031 tax deferred exchanges.

The most common approach to pooling investors funds to purchase larger properties is with a syndication. A syndication has a sponsor or general partner (I will use those terms interchangeably) and investors or limited partners. The sponsors find and underwrite the deal, do all the work to purchase and manage the property, and put together the framework of the investment. The investors contribute funds and make returns.

In the U.S., syndications are typically structured as private placement offerings. These are special exemptions in the U.S. securities code that allow you to create and market a security privately without all the immense amount of paperwork involved in a public offering. There are many rules. I won't go over all of them; just know that there are rules about who can invest in a syndication, how you can market one, how much money you can raise, etc.

Because syndications are private offerings, the biggest challenge has always been connecting sponsors with investors. You literally have to already know someone before they can offer you a security. Recent changes in the securities laws have made it easier to find some types of investors (so-called 'accredited investors' who have a net worth over $1 million, not including their personal residence or have income over $250,000 per year). But challenges remain.

Also, because syndications are private and individual, the approach to managing the syndication is often ad hoc. How is ownership managed? How are distributions made? How do the sponsors communicate with investors? There are no rules. There are platforms that provide software and sites that help with this management, but using that software is an extra cost to the sponsor (worth it, but still an extra cost). Many sponsors just use their own home-grown processes to handle the property and investor management.

It can be complicated to manage a syndication. Most of them do not allow investors to buy or sell while the investment is in operation. Usually, the investors invest before the sponsors close on the property and their money is tied up until the property is sold, often five to seven years later. There is little to no liquidity of the investment. Some rules may prohibit investors from selling their investment for the first year. And they may only be able to sell to an accredited investor. It is also common that the sponsors have first right of refusal to buy investor interest and that sponsors must approve the new buyer. Many of these challenges apply to DSTs and TICs equally as well as syndications.

Whew. Yes, it's complicated, but compared to a public offering it's a walk in the park. Syndications are the main way that sponsors pool investors' funds to purchase larger properties. With all its challenges, it has been the best way to go. Until now.

Security Token Offerings

Security Token Offerings (STOs) started almost accidentally. Many of the initial coin offerings in 2017 were, for all intents and purposes, ownership of the company issuing the ICO. The company would publish a white paper of the cool, new software they were creating that was going to solve some immense problem. The profits from the software would accrue to the token holders. Many of these companies created the tokens without any understanding of securities laws. But clearly their tokens satisfied all the elements of the Howey Test—they were *investments of money* in a *common enterprise* with an *expectation of profit* due *solely to the efforts of the company creators and employees*. Bingo. They are a security.

Unfortunately, many of these companies did not follow the requirements for creating a security, and many were shut down by the SEC. Some were required to return investor funds, and many were fined. These issues continue today—the SEC often works slowly. The cryptocurrency Ripple was only declared to be a security in December 2020.

But out of all this chaos, it became clear that as long as you followed the security laws—you created a private placement memorandum, took care in how the tokens were sold, and you registered the security as exempt under one of the SEC regulations (typically Regulation D or Regulation S)—you could issue tokens that were ownership in a company. It was still much easier than a typical syndication. Also, around this time, the SEC opened up new avenues for reaching investors. If you set your syndication up under Regulation D as a 506C exemption, you could only sell to accredited investors, but you could advertise publicly. If you stayed with a Reg D 506B, you could allow a certain number of non-accredited investors in your deal, but you could not advertise publicly. Lastly, new approaches to Regulation A and crowd funding were allowed. These syndications took longer to set up but they allowed you to advertise and sell to the general public—though the amount you could raise was often limited.

That's a lot of alphabet soup: Reg A, Reg D, Reg S. But the upshot was that you could create tokens that represented ownership in assets (in this case companies) and sell them legally in the U.S. It was a short step from there to creating tokens that were backed by other types of assets. Tokens have been created to own valuable paintings. Tokens have been created backed by gold. And, more importantly for our purposes, tokens are starting to be created that are backed by real estate. We call this process property tokenization. You can look at this two ways. In one way you have a property and you tokenize the ownership of it so that many people can own small pieces of the ownership (note that you are not subdividing the property; everyone owns the whole thing just as a share). The other way to look at it is that you have created a token that is backed by a real asset. The result is the same, but your starting point changes.

STOs make cryptocurrency bleed over into the real world. In some sense, STOs are like shares in a private placement memorandum (PPM). In some cases, STOs might act like a TIC. But now you have combined the flexibility and ease of use of cryptocurrency with the more traditional ways of investing in larger real estate deals. As we shall see, this is a revolution in real estate investing that, as of 2021, is just beginning. Today only a handful of STOs tokenizing real estate exist. But with the proof of concept done, there is no question this approach will take off. I predict that five years from now all syndications will be implemented as STOs.

There are some complications in putting STOs on the blockchain. Several approaches are now competing for attention and use. Understanding some of the critical issues involved will help you to better decide how to evaluate the offerings.

Public vs. Private Blockchains and Sidechains

Properly implemented STOs are self-enforcing smart contracts that automatically implement the SEC regulations and regulations from other countries. STOs are global, after all, and ideally will comply with the securities regulations of all the countries relevant to the offering. These smart contract rules can't be stored on most public blockchains. If you think about it, this makes sense. Most blockchains are designed to store transactions. If you start filling them with large amounts of data, you can fit fewer transactions in a block, which dramatically cuts your transaction speed. The blockchains have to put limits on what you can do.

This fact leaves you two choices. The first is to create a private blockchain where you can store exactly the data you want. You manage the blockchain and own it. Many of the STO service creators have taken this approach, as it is easier and gives the service more control. However, this is a private blockchain. All of the instances of the blockchain are owned and managed by the service (or by you in some cases). Several important features of the blockchain that we have started to take for granted with Bitcoin are no longer present. Transactions are no longer immutable; since you have control of all instances, you can just replace them with whatever you want. And if a company that manages its own blockchain goes out of business, what happens to the blockchain? What happens to the assets? Unless otherwise prepared for, they disappear. Private blockchains do not have the immutability and security of the prominent public blockchains.

The other way to handle the issue is to split the information in the smart contract. The transactions (buys, sells, trades, sends, ownership) are held on a public blockchain, and the detailed smart contract information is held on a separate, usually private, blockchain. Thus, the key fact of ownership is immutable, and only the other details are at risk. It may be easier to recreate the tokens on another platform if a company were to go out of business. And while the company could change its private blockchain, it couldn't affect the ownership.

These private blockchains connected tightly to public blockchains are sometimes called sidechains. And there is a very strong history of storing associated information to a transaction outside the primary blocks. Virtually all blockchains do it now to maintain transaction speeds while supporting richer information storage.

When selecting a provider who will create the STO, make sure that at least the ownership and transaction information is stored on one of the primary public blockchains. You can count on the transactions being immutable and your ownership being safer because of that.

STO Components and Provider Types

When you create a STO, there are several components that have to be addressed. While many services are being created, most only address a few of the components. You should make sure anyone you work with can handle what you need to have handled and that the combined services give you a complete solution. Here are the main components of what you need to legally create and operate a STO:

- Private Placement Memorandum: Yes, this is the same PPM you would have to do for a syndication. You have to have this to comply with SEC regulations. Your PPM will rely on one of the SEC exemptions and must be registered. These documents typically have dozens of pages of 'risks' describing anything that can go wrong. Your securities attorney—the person who creates a PPM—will need to add risks specific to cryptocurrency and STOs.
- KYC and AML processes and documentation: These processes ensure you know who is investing in the deal by buying the cryptocurrency and check that you are not laundering funds. Typically, you will have an online platform where an investor can provide her information and you can check against

the appropriate databases. The KYC and AML info provided and the results of your checks have to be maintained in case you have to prove you followed the rules.

- The token itself: Creating a token is really easy. Anyone can create one in a few minutes. Creating a token that can automatically enforce securities regulations on exchanges and combines a sidechain and a public blockchain is much more challenging. Fortunately, virtually every STO company does this. You will find that everyone who claims to be in the STO business provides this part in one way or another.

- Token management: These systems allow you to track the ownership of the STOs so you can provide distributions, allow investors to vote (when required as part of the PPM), and comply with any legal orders.

- A token exchange: In addition to having the token created, you need a place where it can be bought and sold. Preferably, you can buy directly with fiat currency, but being able to buy with Bitcoin and Ethereum is almost as good. An exchange with no one on it is functionally okay, but you really want an exchange where your token may be available to lots of investors. The ideal is to have a platform with many STOs so your investors can move investments and other investors can buy yours.

In an ideal world, you could find all of the above in one place. But in practice, that's really hard. Few of the companies in this space can provide everything you need. Most of the platforms belong to one of three types:

The first is what I think of as the front end of the STO system. They will require you to find your own lawyer to create your securities documents. But then they will provide the KYC/AML, the token creation, and the token management process on their platform. As rules change, their platform will evolve, and your tokens will keep up. What these providers don't give you is the exchange and the ability to do secondary sales for your investors.

The second type is much the same as the first, except that instead of allowing you to create a token in their platform, they give you your own platform where you can create as many different STOs as you want. These are called 'White Label' platforms since they are generic until you apply your own branding. The white label platform is not just a specific STO. It is a STO generation platform. It will allow you to create as many individual STO currencies as you want for different projects. The cost of the platform (which can be quite expensive) may be amortized across multiple property tokenizations. In fact, you must make multiple STOs in order to make the cost of the platform feasible. It would be too expensive for just one STO.

The third type of platform is the peer-to-peer exchange where multiple STOs can be traded among investors. These platforms create a secondary market for your STOs and dramatically increase your liquidity. These platforms work much like fund raising platforms that aren't on the blockchain. To get an account on the platform, an investor has to provide all her KYC/AML information so that they can qualify to trade. Because that work is done upfront, a sponsor can rely on the fact that anyone who is on the platform is eligible to invest. These peer-to-peer trading exchanges can support automated sales that still comply with securities regulations. Or they can enforce other sales restrictions (like the sponsor being required to approve sales).

The closest I have seen to a STO company that provides end-to-end capability as of 2021 is https://Securitize.com and https://Solidblock.com. Another leader in the field is Polymath. But there are now dozens of companies, each creating their own take on how to do a STO. Many of them use private blockchains, and almost none of them have any capability for peer-to-peer transactions. The company that assembles a full investor platform with KYC and AML checks, token creation, and peer-to-peer trading of STOs is going to really clean up.

The most prominent company in this space tokenizing companies is Securitize. Solidblock, on the other hand, is focused solely on tokenizing real estate. They completed the first real estate property tokenization in 2018 (Aspencoin). It tokenized a hotel in Aspen, Colorado. They currently have a marketplace with several tokenization offerings in progress. They also provide an end-to-end capability from PPM to marketplace and are adding financial services and other support services soon. They are a good bet for serious syndicators looking to make the leap to tokenization.

Earlier in this chapter I said that I believe STOs will largely replace current syndication approaches over the next five years. Five years may be an aggressive estimate, but the advantages of STOs over traditional syndications are many and substantial. In the competitive world of investments, a framework with so many advantages and virtually no disadvantages is bound to outcompete the standard approach. At some point it will be the normal way of doing business, and anyone not doing a STO will be at a disadvantage in raising funds from investors. Early adopters—like you?—will be the ones to transform real estate ownership.

STO Advantages

The biggest advantage to real estate investors of creating a STO to pool investor funds is liquidity. Syndications are attractive investments for all the reasons we have discussed. They allow investors with less capital to own part of large, professionally managed real estate. But syndications have two big challenges: investors must commit their funds for an indefinite period that is often five to 10 years, and it is difficult for an investor to learn about and connect with opportunities because they are private placements. Crypto-currency in the form of STOs solves both of these problems. Peer-to-peer exchanges that enforce all the global securities laws will allow eligible investors to browse investments from around the world and buy and sell their shares, or part of their shares, when they need to.

A second advantage of investing in a STO backed by real estate is the immutability of the transaction and the transparency of owner-ship. Any STO investor can examine the blockchain and see how many investors hold the STO and their relative stakes (they will not know the names of the investors, only the unique wallet addresses that own the tokens). This information provides additional comfort that shares have not been double sold. Remember the play and movie *The Producers*, in which Max Bialystock, the main producer, sold far more than 100% of the ownership of his play? That can't happen with a STO.

The biggest advantages to real estate syndicators of using STOs as their method of creating and managing ownership is access to investors from around the world (provided they have structured their syndications to take advantage of it). STOs solve the problem of meeting and connecting with investors. In addition, the smart contract aspect of STOs simplifies management of investors and assists with everything from cash distributions to sales to provid-ing notices and supporting investor voting. These functions are provided by special purpose platforms now, but STOs provide these capabilities as a matter of course.

Investing in STOs also provides numerous advantages to crypto-currency investors that are unavailable through other types of cryptocurrency. STOs should have little volatility but will likely increase in price as the real estate value increases. They will pay fiat currency dividends, providing the investor cash flow. Very few, if any, cryptocurrencies provide actual income to their investors. Their investment will be backed by a hard asset rather than a white paper and a promise. If everything were to fall apart, the property could be sold and the proceeds distributed to the STO owners. Really, the value of the STO cannot go to nothing as is not only possible but likely with many cryptocurrencies.

And the disadvantages of STOs? There are very few. Right now, many real estate investors are unfamiliar with cryptocurrency. Obtaining ownership with a STO might be confusing and may dissuade some real estate investors from investing. However, the idea that their interest is captured in an immutable fashion, and the fact that they may be able to better manage their investments due to the liquidity of STOs, will ultimately overcome any of these objections.

The other principal disadvantage of having your real estate interest realized by a STO is the potential for losing your tokens by losing your password. However, the use of third-party cryptocurrency holders eliminates this issue. They are responsible for managing the cryptocurrency, just as stockbrokers today are responsible for holding and trading stocks and bonds.

This is an exciting time in real estate investing. The SEC has liberalized some of the more restrictive rules on creating and advertising syndications. And the advent of the Security Token Offering promises a new world where all the advantages of syndications are preserved and their main disadvantages removed.

Imagine that, as an investor, you can create an account on a large peer-to-peer cryptocurrency exchange that focuses on STOs. You can browse private placements from around the world, obtain investor documents, and perform your due diligence on the investment. You can buy from your chair and, once you have passed through any prohibited sales period, you can sell all or part of your investment for fiat currency or cryptocurrencies like Bitcoin, Ethereum, or TROPTIONS. You might even be able to directly trade your ownership in one property for ownership in another. You could argue (and undoubtedly some will) that such an exchange would actually be like kind. We'll see how that shakes out over the next few years.

The STO is a real estate investing technique that is poised to transform how real estate is owned. Not only can it be used to replace how syndications are managed, but it opens up additional tokenization opportunities. Will people tokenize their homes, retaining some ownership but using investors instead of banks to fund their purchase or refinance? Will small businesses raise capital by selling part of their offices, using their capital as a credit line to smooth their cashflow? In that case, they would control the 'interest rate' distribution on the cryptocurrency. The opportunities are endless. The real estate investor who understands STOs will have many more ways to invest, profit, and own real estate.

Summary

Cryptocurrency is poised to change the way real estate is owned by creating mechanisms to tokenize properties and allow many people to own parts of larger properties.

Crypto may take the place of existing forms of pooled ownership like TICs, DSTs, and syndications. In fact, security token offerings are an alternative way of implementing a syndication that provides substantial benefits like improved liquidity to the investor, better compliance with securities regulations, and better access to global markets for private issuers.

STOs are so new and changing so rapidly, it will be challenging to stay up to date. I have created a newsletter where I will provide continuous updates on the progress and ever-changing landscape of STOs (find it at https://CryptoREBook.com). I will keep you up to date on the regulations, the companies that provide services to create and manage STOs, as well as the main players in the security token space.

CHAPTER NINE

REAL ESTATE RECORDS ON THE BLOCKCHAIN

I N THIS BOOK, I have emphasized the role of cryptocurrency in transforming deal-making and now ownership through STOs. But the underlying technology of cryptocurrency, the blockchain, can itself transform ownership of real estate.

At its most basic, the blockchain is a distributed database where chained blocks of data (thus the name blockchain) use cryptography to ensure the records' integrity. When the blockchain is publicly maintained by independent parties, the transactions and ownership of 'tokens' are immutable. For assets as valuable as real estate, where the ownership is slow changing and extremely important to get right, what better approach than the blockchain to record and store that ownership?

In fact, there are numerous real estate records that must be maintained forever. Whole industries have been created to manage these records, insure that they are accurate (yes I do mean insure, not ensure), and to correct them when they are not. These records must be immutable. They should be public so that anyone can know who owns the real estate and so that rights can readily be ascertained and proven. Ideally, the records should be inexpensive to maintain and inexpensive to record. The blockchain provides all of these capabilities and provides them far better than current methods.

The most obvious real estate record to put on the blockchain is real estate title (ownership). In its current state, title records are challenging to search and there is the potential that some long-lost relative from 100 years ago might make a claim on the title and take ownership away from you. It's rare, but it happens.

The reasons for title claims are many and varied, but they either revolve around a loss of records in the past or a new violation like an encroachment on property from a neighbor. When records used to be paper (as they still are in some places), a fire could destroy the official copies. Even as records have become computerized, there are entry errors, unreadable scans, and misfiled or misattributed records. Replacing these with a blockchain-based system can't correct errors of the past but can ensure that records going forward are accurate and protected from inadvertent changes. By using digital smart contracts, human errors will be reduced (the smart contracts would verify against previous blocks and could perform sanity checks on the accuracy of the new transactions).

For new violations of title, being able to easily access boundaries and the geographic coordinates they represent can minimize disagreements and allow for effective enforcement of title.

Title itself can be complicated. In addition to basic title that shows who owns a property, records related to title, such as liens against the property and easements associated with it, could also be maintained. And multiple types of ownership (like mineral rights or air rights) could also be recorded and tracked.

In current systems, you usually can't just look up the records to see who owns a property (often the tax assessor will have that information, but those records are less official). Instead, you have to review all the recorded documents and sequence them in time to figure out ownership. With a cryptocurrency-/blockchain-based approach, you should be able to look up who has all the various ownership categories as well as looking up any and all transactions.

One of the reasons title may be at risk is that any individual record can be changed (legally or illegally) with no inherent method of ensuring the records are the actual ones that were input at the time. With a blockchain, changing one record would change the cryptographic hash for all title records. You couldn't change the title records without it impacting every real estate ownership. This feature (the immutability of transactions) provides strong protection against alteration of past real estate title records. Once records are on a blockchain—provided no pre-blockchain claims are recognized—there might be less need (possibly even no need) for title insurance. There certainly would be no need for expensive title searches. Anyone could effectively complete a title search in an easy and straightforward manner.

Even the government itself would be unable to alter past records if the blockchain was maintained publicly. Publicly maintained records could provide stronger property rights in jurisdictions subject to corruption. Countries or states that wanted to increase the confidence investors would feel investing in their locations could move title to the blockchain. It may be an approach that would attract more investment.

Several jurisdictions have piloted programs to put title on the blockchain. Cook County in Illinois was one of the first. And the Georgian Government has launched a program to put all real estate title in that nation on the blockchain. The United Kingdom (UK) and

Zambia are also piloting programs. Ideally, a global system could be developed that would allow property ownership anywhere in the world to be searched. It would not require that all countries use the same system, just that they use systems with compatible cryptocurrency token standards.

Beyond Title – Additional Records on the Blockchain

Going beyond title, there are other real estate records that could be stored on the blockchain. Contracts for real estate sales or leases could be created as digital contracts and stored on a blockchain. Several companies have developed systems for contract collaboration, execution, and automatic enforcement. The first iterations of contracts on the blockchain were merely scanned PDF documents. But the latest systems actually digitize the contract elements (buyer, seller, property, title type, etc.) so that those elements can have well determined and common meanings.

Smart contracts are different from most cryptocurrencies. Most cryptocurrencies are fungible. But smart contracts are unique. They are non-fungible and can't be exchanged. In fact, while the contract itself may be immutable (once signed), the details of the token information may only be accessed by the parties. It provides the best of both worlds. Anyone can know a contract exists but only the parties can access the details.

Once title and contracts are on the blockchain, many more possibilities present themselves. There are many other legal documents or information about a property that should be maintained for long periods of time. Documents such as zoning and zoning variances, grandfathered uses, and conditional use permits could be stored with the property so that owners could prove their allowed uses. Building permits and inspections could be stored on a blockchain. Business licenses that attach to a property rather than an owner could be stored. Tax liens and any other tax records like home-stead exemptions and tax appraisals could be stored attached to the property on a blockchain.

An entire property profile could be created so that legal property information that is public and should be maintained and protected is available for easy search using a common blockchain explorer. This information would also be easy to deconflict and reduce errors in approvals for zoning applications or tax assessments.

Property owners who are selling could formalize much of their due diligence information on the blockchain providing potential buyers or investors easier access and greater confidence in the information. These records might be better on a private blockchain and treated as short term but immutable while they are active.

Putting property records, especially title, on the blockchain has the potential to transform ownership by making the various types of ownership transparent and publicly searchable. By making the records immutable, the blockchain can increase investment. As an example, in Zambia the properties that have title secured on a blockchain have their values increase around 10% just from the reliability of title.

Whole industries are devoted to title. There are title companies whose main job is to search and verify title. There are title insurance companies that insure against the rare event of a claim against title and the much more common infringement of title (your neighbor builds their garage partially on your land). Both of these industries will be impacted by title on the blockchain.

The promise of global title, where an investor can know the ownership of any property in the world, is intriguing. Combine that with the ability of cryptocurrency to make international payments quickly and transparently, and you have a complete transformation of international real estate investing.

Summary

Real estate records like title, easements, ground leases, and liens can be recorded on a blockchain as smart contracts. Once the records are on the blockchain they are public, easily searched, and immutable. Putting these records on a blockchain can make real estate ownership and investing much easier and faster. It will reduce risk from title claims and can even increase property values in areas of the world where corruption calls current record keeping into question.

Beyond recording the public records, it is possible to record all types of property information on the blockchain. This would create an immutable property profile that will help owners and investors to know with certainty the zoning exceptions, property status, and other legal information about a property.

If standards are followed for recording title on the blockchain, it may be possible for an investor to search title of any property in any country from anywhere in the world.

SECTION IV

TRANSFORMING MANAGEMENT

CHAPTER TEN

UTILITY TOKENS FOR REAL ESTATE

I N ADDITION TO TRANSFORMING deal-making and ownership in real estate, cryptocurrency also has a novel role to play in real estate management.

Many people think of real estate as the physical property, but often, real estate has a business component to it. Apartments are property but they support a rental business. Hotels are accommodations businesses. Assisted living is real estate with a very intense business component that includes providing assistance and care. And any business can find ways to use cryptocurrency to improve their customers' experiences, increase loyalty, and build relationships.

There are two primary ways to use cryptocurrency in a real estate business. The first is to accept cryptocurrency as payment for your business services. I will cover that in the next chapter. The other way is to create your own cryptocurrency and use that within your business to support your customer base and improve your customer relationships. Most of these techniques involve using your cryptocurrency as a utility token.

As you will recall from Chapter 1, a utility token is a token that is issued by a business and used to pay for goods or services within that business. It might not be obvious how this applies to real estate businesses. It will help to look at similar approaches that businesses have taken that don't involve cryptocurrency or the blockchain. I will use these historical analogs to suggest ideas for how to use crypto in your real estate business.

Customer Loyalty Programs

Going way back to the 60s and 70s, many companies issued something called green stamps. When you checked out at the register, you would be issued these stamps (yes, they were actual stamps like postage stamps). You would then paste them into a book of stamps. When a book was full, you could trade it in for goods. This was unwieldy and sticky, and a real pain to do (though as a kid I guess pasting the stamps into a book kept me busy and out of my grandma's hair for a while). But it felt like you were getting something for free. And you would go back to those retailers who issued the green stamps instead of retailers that didn't. You were getting something extra.

Today there are many programs that are designed to build customer loyalty. Airlines have frequent-flyer programs. Hotels and car rental agencies allow you to earn points, as do credit cards. To a very limited extent, some of these points transfer between businesses that have agreements amongst themselves. These programs work exactly like utility tokens and could be better implemented as utility tokens.

Why have these companies implemented these programs? The short answer is that they work. When your industry is a commodity like airline flights or hotels, it is important to create a reason why customers should choose you over your competitors. Customer loyalty is especially important for travel-related companies. The customer often has no experience with the specific hotel and can only go by the niche of the hotel and its brand. Within the same niche, the brands are more alike than different. But a loyalty program that can get you upgrades, free flights, or stays or rental days, can encourage a particular customer to go out of their way to work with a particular company. It is more effective from a customer's point of view to build points with one company than to spread them out among multiple companies. They get free stuff faster that way.

These loyalty programs provide numerous benefits both to the companies and to the customers. From the company's side, the programs build bonds and relationships with their customers. The customers have a stake in the company by holding those points. The points themselves also have a perceived value—even though on most of the sites they explicitly state that the points have no cash value.

As a customer builds points, she gets treated better. She may be allowed to board early or avoid extra bag fees on an airplane. At a hotel, she may get access to special lounges or get a turndown service in her room. She achieves levels usually named for precious metals and at each level gets additional perks. Many of the perks are inexpensive and just result in being treated better. You could argue it would make more sense to just treat everyone better. But large companies that treat many of their customers badly can focus their energy on people who continually reuse their services and get a stable base of income from these frequent flyers.

But utility tokens can take these loyalty programs to the next level. Most loyalty programs are difficult to use, have all kinds of restrictions, and are poorly managed. The poor management is largely because all the programs are unique to the company. A company has to maintain its own software with its own rules and authentication. It has to track the loyalty points, apply them to sales (while also applying the whole rat's nest of restrictions), and allow them to expire. Some of this complexity is undoubtedly intended to discourage the actual use of points while simultaneously advertising the heck out of how good they are.

Utility tokens have lots of advantages for customers over existing loyalty programs. They are assets, potentially have value, and could be sold. In fact, the value of utility tokens used in loyalty programs could increase as the cost of flights increases. These attributes give customers more control over their points. They give the company more perceived value of their loyalty program. But they do give customers a chance to switch loyalties, which for some programs could defeat the purpose.

But the mechanics of utility tokens are much better for both companies and customers. Because utility tokens are cryptocurrency, they are immutable, can't be double spent, and can't be counterfeited or forged. Current programs constantly have to maintain their computer-security profiles. A hacker who could add a million miles to an account could fly for free for a long time. And cryptocurrency would be much simpler to manage. All the actual management of the tokens would be handled by the blockchain and by cryptocurrency exchanges. All the company has to do is issue utility tokens to customers and accept them for payment.

Implementing Loyalty Programs for Real Estate

How would cryptocurrency-based loyalty programs work for real estate businesses? The answer is twofold. The first piece is the mechanics of the program and how to implement it. The second is the business case for how it is used within the real estate business and what kinds of services or goods it buys. Throughout the discussion, I will use an example of a student housing property, but similar approaches could work for other types of apartments and for other types of real estate.

How do you implement a utility token? There are four main steps:

- Creating the cryptocurrency: This task is actually quite easy. Anyone can create a new cryptocurrency in just a few minutes and at no cost. The real work here is deciding which public blockchain your cryptocurrency will be recorded on. Making that decision is beyond the scope of this book. But here are a few considerations: 1) the popularity of the blockchain—will it be around years from now? 2) transaction speed and cost—every blockchain will have differences in how large blocks are, how often they are recorded, and how the transaction fees vary 3) token standards—many tokens are ERC-20 compliant. You should just check to make sure it isn't something odd 4) initial value—you will have to identify an initial value for the cryptocurrency. If someone wanted to buy it from you, what would you charge? This is important because it will affect how much you issue to customers and what they redeem it for.

- Issuing the cryptocurrency: You will need to determine how your customers earn the cryptocurrency. One method I like is for each customer to be awarded cryptocurrency for each *on-time* monthly payment. Yes, you have now provided a carrot for on-time payments as well as the stick of a late fee. You might even provide the cryptocurrency only if they pay by the 1st of the month, where the late fee applies only after the 5th. You could issue cryptocurrency as a referral fee either in addition to cash or in place of cash. You could issue cryptocurrency for early renewals. Really, any behavior you want to incentivize could be encouraged by issuing an appropriate amount of cryptocurrency. Think about how credit card companies issue extra points if you spend a target amount of dollars in a specific time period.

- Managing the cryptocurrency: There is really very little to do in managing the cryptocurrency. Once you have a cryptocurrency on a blockchain, all the transaction capability is taken care of with the exception of small amounts of cryptocurrency to pay for transactions. But there are some issues here with how you provide the cryptocurrency to your customers. I recommend creating wallets for each of your customers and issuing the cryptocurrency to those wallets. You can provide the passphrase (or password) to the wallets to your customers, but keep a copy so you can assist your less technologically capable customers with any transactions. Your customers can create their own wallets and move their tokens to those wallets if they choose and want more privacy. But then they would be responsible for any transaction fees to redeem the cryptocurrency. As long as they leave the cryptocurrency in the wallets you create, you can assist them with redemption. You can provide them a link that allows them to view their wallet and the amount of cryptocurrency they have. With this approach, issuing is simple: just send cryptocurrency to their wallet. Redeeming is also simple. They can ask you to redeem, and you can add the right amount of crypto to their wallet to pay the transaction fee and send it back to you. If they have their own wallet, they can just send the crypto to your wallet address.

- Redeeming the cryptocurrency: Lastly, you need to be able to redeem the cryptocurrency (accept it for payment) for a good or service. This can be a simple affair where you verify the send back to your wallet and the address it came from. Or you could use a more sophisticated point of sale approach. The key is to have a price list for the things your clients can buy.

Why Loyalty Programs for Real Estate

Besides the nuts and bolts of implementation, there should be a business case for how you use cryptocurrency. There are a few principals here that should be kept in mind. First, the cryptocurrency should be issued to encourage behavior that you want your customers to display. On-time payments of rent is a prime example. But other good behaviors, like referrals of other customers or early lease renewal, are good candidates. You could reward longevity of being a customer on some sort of sliding scale. As an example, you might provide cryptocurrency worth around $10/month for the first year, $15/month for the second, and $20/month for all the ensuing years. Any behavior could be rewarded (if you are trying to incentivize showing up at events you could even reward attendance).

Even more fun is the variety of ways that cryptocurrency could be redeemed. Many good property managers reward loyalty with additional amenities or perks to their residents. By formalizing this with cryptocurrency, you create a culture where your residents count on the cryptocurrency to get free stuff. And the cryptocurrency may be worthless elsewhere. They won't want to lose what they've saved. This fact results in increased loyalty that can be tangibly measured by the amount of cryptocurrency your tenants have.

Now suppose your competitor tries to defuse this loyalty program by also accepting your cryptocurrency for payment (this could happen if your program is wildly successful). How great is that? You get to issue it—only you can and only your residents can earn it—but your competitor has to pay for the redemption! You could then start actually selling the cryptocurrency to their residents and they have to redeem it. You now have a new income stream.

Here is a short list of items your customers could buy from you with the cryptocurrency. To keep this list manageable, I will focus only on the student housing property example:

- Rent: They could save their cryptocurrency for a couple of years and get a month's free rent
- Amenities like a ceiling fan or rent of a washer and dryer or upgrade/replacement of carpet
- Use cryptocurrency to run washers and dryers in the laundry room
- Clubhouse or pool reservation for a party
- Payment of a late fee
- Bicycle rental or rental of a moving van
- Pet fee payment
- Valet trash payment .

There are many potential income streams at a student housing property and at other properties. Allowing your customers to select their 'free' stuff is a great way of building brand loyalty, retaining tenants, and making use of some of your facility's features. Many of these options actually cost your business nothing, as they are payment for something the customer might not have used without the cryptocurrency. The cryptocurrency could be enough to get your customers into a trial period after which they will be paying extra to keep the amenity. Some of these are additional income streams. You will have to balance the loss of additional income against the value of the extra loyalty. You don't want to harm your overall income to put a loyalty program in place.

Especially for something like student housing, a cryptocurrency-based loyalty program will have a cool factor that could set you apart from all of your competitors. A senior housing apartment complex might not be as good a place for such a program, but student housing, self-storage, other apartments, and hospitality would be great businesses to incorporate such a program.

Savings Programs Using Cryptocurrency

Another way of incorporating utility tokens to manage your business is with a savings program. A loyalty program is focused on current customers and increasing their loyalty to your business. A savings program is focused on future customers, tying them to your business early on before they need it. A savings program may not be applicable to as many real estate businesses as a loyalty program, but there are several businesses where it may really make sense.

A savings program is implemented in much the same way as a loyalty program, with one major difference. Generally, the crypto is purchased with fiat by future customers. Often there are small regular sales over time so that the cryptocurrency accumulates. Think of paying a hundred dollars a month on autopay and buying cryptocurrency with it to store in a wallet. Over five or ten years (or longer) a substantial amount of cryptocurrency could be accumulated that could be used within the business. The price will vary over time, but for an appreciating cryptocurrency (as this would be), the regular savings works similar to dollar cost averaging in buying stocks or bonds.

The critical piece of making this work for both the customer and the business owner is that the cost of services is fixed in terms of the cryptocurrency. For example, if cryptocurrency is used as rent, the cost of the rent denominated in cryptocurrency is always the same (for example, it always takes 500 rent tokens to pay rent) while the cost of the rent in dollars may increase, perhaps substantially. This factor also means that the value of the cryptocurrency rises over time as dollar denominated rents rise. In fact, for a utility token used in this fashion, the value of the cryptocurrency (and its cost when purchased) is 1/500 times the current asking rent.

Why does this work for everyone? For the customer, they get a return on their investment because the first 500 tokens they buy may be much less than the rent while the last 500 tokens they buy are exactly the rent cost. They get predictability in the number of months of rent they can afford when they finally need the business' services. Alternatively, they will get a lower rent for a longer time by using the cryptocurrency for part of the rent. Lastly, customers in the savings program may be given priority for selection to fill vacancies. It provides another type of certainty.

For the business owner, this approach provides rent far in advance of actual costs of the renter living at the property. That income can be invested—ideally at a rate greater than the rent increases—providing the business owner an additional income stream that more than covers the ultimate cost. The savings program also creates a very strong tie to your business. There is little doubt that the customer is going to use your services when the time comes and will likely need to augment the cryptocurrency to pay the rent (unless they have been saving for a long time). And if the customer does not use your services, you have received their funds and need provide nothing in return directly to them. But since the savings are cryptocurrency, the customer may be able to sell it to one of your other customers.

The savings program also allows the business owner to increase their market demographic. You can market not just to customers who need you now but who need you in the future. This is easier to understand by looking at specific real estate businesses where a savings program could make sense.

One of those is assisted living. The costs of a quality assisted living facility can be substantial, as much as $10,000/month, though the average is closer to $3,800/month. To prepare for these costs, some people buy long-term care insurance. Having an insurance program that will foot the bill is a good idea. Long-term care insurance policies are broad and apply at any assisted living facility. But they can be expensive. And many people just don't plan that far ahead.

A lower cost and more focused option would be to purchase a cryptocurrency savings program issued by an assisted living facility that can be used to pay the monthly rates. This could be a savings program on autopay where each month money is deducted from the customer's account and used to purchase cryptocurrency at the current market price. Over time, the amount of cryptocurrency saved would help to cover the costs of the assisted living home.

This type of program works better when the person already has a good idea which assisted living home she may want to move into. Markets where your home stands out as the best, or businesses that have multiple homes may make the best choices for these programs. And many people are accustomed to saving for retirement. This marketing approach will undoubtedly make your home stand out from the crowd.

Another business where the future need is obvious well in advance is for student housing. As with saving for retirement, parents are accustomed to saving for college. And many are locked into college savings programs for a particular college or university. Saving a little more so that their child can have their pick of student housing is a natural extension to these programs. Ensuring a sibling can also live at the best student housing is something parents can get behind. Over the longer term, you may even have parents wanting their children to follow their legacy, not just to a particular college but a particular housing site.

Cryptocurrency savings programs are also ideal for parents or grandparents to assist their children as they are starting out in their new apartment. Gift cards are used everywhere in retail. There is no reason not to use them in real estate. It is much less awkward than having those wanting to contribute pay part of the rent. And the parents may want to make sure any money given to their children is used for rent. A cryptocurrency savings program would work well to implement a gift card program.

One additional benefit of a savings program from the business's point of view is the insight it gives them into their customer base. A business will know (or should know and track) how many future customers are saving and when they are likely to require services. This information allows the business to better plan for expansion and could make it easier to obtain debt or investment for that expansion. It may be the closest thing to a crystal ball a business can have.

Summary

Loyalty programs and savings programs implemented as cryptocurrency utility tokens are promising methods poised to transform how real estate is managed. These types of programs have been very successful for the travel industry and credit cards, but they can be implemented better on a blockchain. Investors who are the first to start these programs will get the most attention and could make a big impact in their markets. There is a novelty to this approach that will gain attention. But behind the novelty are solid business motives and exciting new incentives for your customers. Exploiting those will create win-win situations for everyone.

CHAPTER ELEVEN

ACCEPTING CRYPTOCURRENCY FOR PAYMENT

A NOTHER WAY THAT CRYPTOCURRENCY can transform the way you manage your business is to incorporate it into your payment processing. You can accept cryptocurrency for payment for all or part of your services. In the previous chapter I discussed creating your own cryptocurrency that you accept as payment as a way of implementing loyalty or savings programs. In this chapter, I discuss accepting other cryptocurrency.

This doesn't mean that you should accept just any cryptocurrency. Chances are you will choose to accept the more popular (and more liquid) crypto, possibly just Bitcoin. You may also decide to accept other coins or tokens that meet your own investment criteria or that meet other strategic business needs.

Accepting cryptocurrency for your goods and services will put you in the vanguard of businesses moving into the future. As accepting crypto becomes easier and more socially and financially acceptable, there will come a point when not accepting cryptocurrency will be a serious disadvantage to businesses. Now, in 2021, however, businesses that accept cryptocurrency are the exception. Accepting crypto will make your business stand out among your competition. Today there are over 70,000 businesses that do accept cryptocurrency for payment, and with new payment methods rapidly being developed and being rolled out, it will only become easier.

Cryptocurrency is poised to join some time-honored approaches to alternate payments. How many apartment complexes provide a free apartment or a reduced rent apartment as part of their employees' compensation? There are many of them. And there are many ways of accounting for that additional compensation. There are gradations of providing services or goods for labor. Some apartment complexes give rent breaks for people who help out around the complex. In this case, the person is not actually an employee, but gets a reduced rent for providing their skills at the complex. This approach in particular is often a barter transaction and 'off the books.' I point all this out to identify existing barter transactions that are generally win-win trades between residents and apartment complex owners.

Accepting cryptocurrency for goods or services in your business can be approached like trading labor for the same goods and services. In those cases, the cryptocurrency acts like a barter transaction, in which you can mutually value the trade in any reasonable way.

As payment systems improve, however, accepting cryptocurrency within your business can be almost exactly like accepting fiat currency. There are numerous payment apps that act as middle men with the cryptocurrency. These apps behave differently, but in general, the customer provides them with cryptocurrency. At time of payment, the app pays your business in fiat (dollars). Later the app coordinates the liquidation of the cryptocurrency and settles up. Many apps will combine multiple sales into bulk transactions to minimize the crypto transaction fees.

Accepting the cryptocurrency then works similarly to accepting credit cards. Your business pays a transaction fee to the app company, which may be a percentage of the transaction amount. But the transaction fees may be much less than similar credit card transaction fees, since overall the crypto transaction fees themselves are much less than banking fees.

Even major payment services are starting to use cryptocurrency. PayPal recently launched a program to store and use cryptocurrency in transactions. As these popular and widely used services normalize the use of cryptocurrency, any business can advertise accepting cryptocurrency in simple and effective ways.

Unlike hotels or office buildings, payment systems for real estate businesses like apartments and self-storage are often much less automated. How many people still pay rent with checks or with automatic withdrawals? But most real estate businesses are now implementing online payments, and those payment systems could accept cryptocurrency rather easily.

There are several ways to deal with accepting cryptocurrency and what to do with the cryptocurrency after you have accepted it. The main approaches are:

- Not accepting the cryptocurrency directly. In this case, you accept a payment system that liquidates the cryptocurrency for you; you actually receive cash. I can't imagine a reason you wouldn't do this. It's just like accepting a credit card. As long as the transaction fees are the same or less than other payment methods (or you can charge a transaction fee on top of your other charges) and as long as the payment company is reputable, this is a no-brainer.

- Accept the cryptocurrency directly but liquidate it immediately. This is a possibility if you accept only the major cryptocurrencies. It will require your business to be crypto savvy and you'll need to know how to use crypto exchanges. There is a risk due to the cryptocurrency volatility, but you can always delay or speed transactions to sell at the volatility top. The volatility can work in your favor as well. This approach truly accepts cryptocurrency (the first approach is really cheating. It's the payment company that is accepting the cryptocurrency). And your business can manage transaction fees (reducing them well below credit card fees) by combining multiple transactions into one liquidation.

- Accept the cryptocurrency and trade it for other assets. This is an interesting approach, especially as barter currencies like TROPTIONS or REXNET become more popular. It moves some of your cash flow income into barter transactions and could provide advantages in managing income and expenses. This would be a time and effort intensive approach, but may have substantial investment advantages.

- Accept the cryptocurrency and keep it in your investment portfolio. This is the most aggressive approach to accepting cryptocurrency. It treats crypto as an investment itself and allows full flexibility in managing that portfolio. Real estate businesses that include investors might even be able to provide cryptocurrency directly as part of their distributions. This provides the same flexibility to their investment portfolios as to the business's portfolio. But there may be a much smaller number of potential investors who would be interested in receiving cryptocurrency as part of their distributions—at least right now. As cryptocurrency becomes more popular, easier to use, and more valuable, providing crypto as part of the distribution could be an attractive and innovative investment vehicle.

Advantages of Accepting Crypto in Your Business

Why would a business decide to accept cryptocurrency for goods and services? There are many advantages. The first is to distinguish your business from all the others out there. Businesses succeed best when they have a distinct image and unique offerings. Right now, any real estate owner who accepts cryptocurrency for rent is going to be distinct. Particular real estate niches, especially student housing or apartments that cater to a younger demographic, are prime candidates. There the cool factor of accepting cryptocurrency could be a substantial advantage over other similar properties.

Other real estate businesses, like self-storage or car washes could also gain market share by being seen as innovative and modern. Uniqueness in a market niche where the real estate is usually viewed as a commodity (aren't all self-storage 10x10 units the same?) can reduce price pressures as well as increase the customer base and customer loyalty.

There are also potential financial advantages of accepting cryptocurrency. Crypto can be an increasing asset (instead of a depreciating asset like fiat currency). It may create an additional income stream to make return from the cryptocurrency over and above the actual rents paid.

There is additional financial flexibility in how and when the value of the cryptocurrency is realized. When all you get is fiat, there is no real discussion about how the income is accrued. You have to obey the rules about recognizing the value and income from cryptocurrency, but those are still in flux and there are multiple approaches—all of which are reasonable—to assessing the value of cryptocurrency.

Challenges to Accepting Cryptocurrency

There are challenges in accepting cryptocurrency for goods and services. Managing cash flow is more difficult if the crypto is not immediately liquid. Many businesses already have cash flow problems. Removing some of the cash from the income may not be the best idea for those businesses.

The volatility of cryptocurrency can be an issue for some businesses as well. If cryptocurrency increases in value, everything is fine, but if cryptocurrency tanks, the loss of value could destroy a business. As long as the amount of cryptocurrency accepted by the business is limited, these issues can be managed, but it is certainly a cautionary tale to avoid accepting cryptocurrency for everything.

Cryptocurrency is unfamiliar. It could be challenging to hire staff who know how to accept and manage cryptocurrency. Most bookkeepers and accountants don't know how to keep the books that include cryptocurrency or to file taxes that include crypto transactions. As cryptocurrency becomes more popular, accountants will have to become more savvy about how to include them. But today there are few accountants that can actually claim experience and knowledge about the alternatives for claiming cryptocurrency as income.

Cryptocurrency is also unfamiliar to other providers who make decisions about your company based on credit or profitability. Lenders may not count income in the form of cryptocurrency unless immediate liquidity can be proven. Investors in the business may be deterred (or in some cases encouraged) by having cryptocurrency as part of the business. But today those who are deterred outnumber those that are encouraged.

Virtually all of these disadvantages to including cryptocurrency are driven by its newness and a lack of familiarity to investors, lenders, accountants, and staff. Once cryptocurrency returns can be shown and there is experience in how to manage crypto as part of business income, one can expect that incorporating crypto will be an advantage when it is a low risk and lucrative addition. Crypto will be considered risky when it is actually risky.

Right now, however, if you can identify those approaches that are actually low-risk and incorporate them into your business, you can out-manage your competitors and gain an advantage through innovation.

Summary

As with deal-making and ownership, cryptocurrency is making inroads into how you manage your real estate businesses. Crypto is an easier, better, and more flexible approach to implementing loyalty and savings programs. Those programs can improve your relationship with your customers and broaden your customer base and income streams. Crypto-based loyalty or savings programs are innovative ways of connecting with customers that take advantage of modern marketing techniques and mimic best-in-class programs like frequent flyer miles or credit card points.

Accepting cryptocurrency as payment for your goods and services is an important step into future financial management. It's more complex than just accepting fiat. There are decisions to be made about how to accept crypto, which cryptocurrencies to accept, and when (if?) to liquidate the cryptocurrency to fiat. But the alternatives open up new options for managing your cash flow and your income stream. A smart real estate investor will find ways to take advantage of these methods to increase her profits from the real estate businesses. These techniques will distinguish you from your competitors in the eyes of your customers and your investors.

Ultimately, combining these cryptocurrency-based management approaches with the ability to construct deals and structure ownership will create synergies in your business. These synergies will improve profits while making your business—and your real estate holdings—more attractive to your customers.

CHAPTER TWELVE

ACTION PLAN FOR INVESTORS

A S YOU HAVE SEEN in this book, there are numerous opportuni-ties to combine real estate and cryptocurrency. You can and should purchase real estate with cryptocurrency (or if you own the real estate, sell for cryptocurrency). You can use security token offerings to tokenize a property and sell partial ownership. And you can apply cryptocurrency to improve your overall business processes in various real estate businesses.

That's a lot to take in. But I will have failed in this book if I don't help you understand what to actually do now. My favorite podcast is *Real Estate Guys Radio*. Their motto is "Education for effective action." I couldn't agree more. In this final chapter, I want to give you some specific actions to take depending on whether you are already a real estate investor or a cryptocurrency investor. The advice also depends greatly on your objectives (all investment advice should) and your resources. And it also depends on your particular risk profile and investment philosophy. There is no one-size-fits-all advice except to learn what you need to know and take action.

As Robert Kiyosaki is fond of saying, investing is a team sport. You don't have to go it alone. There are many resources available to you if you choose to combine real estate and cryptocurrency. Dozens of books are available about real estate investing, and people who can help you learn about real estate investing are available nationally and in every city. Similarly, there are many people who can tell you about cryptocurrency, though most of them are focused on buying and selling cryptocurrency itself—not trading it for assets.

There are very few resources, however, that focus on the nexus between real estate and cryptocurrency. There is a LinkedIn group, the International Blockchain Real Estate Association (IBREA) (https://www.linkedin.com/groups/6540665/). But most resources are scattered. To fill that gap, I have put together some resources specifically focused on the intersection of real estate and cryptocurrency. Among the resources that are available:

- A monthly newsletter with up-to-date developments in real estate and cryptocurrency (sign up at https://CrytpoREBook. com)
- A free video series on real estate / cryptocurrency topics
- Numerous articles in *Think Realty Magazine* about cryptocurrency and real estate (https://thinkrealty.com/think-realty-magazine-archive/)
- A crypto-real estate site with links to articles and additional resources related to cryptocurrency and real estate (also at https://CryptoREBook.com).

It is also possible for me to assist you directly with buying or selling your property for cryptocurrency. I can help through the entire buying or selling process. I can also assist you in setting up your business processes to include cryptocurrency loyalty or savings programs or accepting crypto for your goods or services.

Reach out to me at https://www.streetsmartinvestmentsllc.com for more information or to discuss alternatives.

No, you don't have to do this on your own. But what you do will have to depend on your particular objectives. Are you more interested in cash flow, appreciation, or tax advantages? Are you more concerned with brand loyalty or making your business really cool? If you want cash flow, moving cryptocurrency into real estate could be the approach you want. Or perhaps you would invest in a STO. If your preference is appreciation, converting some of your real estate to cryptocurrency will give you exposure to the most rapidly appreciating asset class in the world. Tax advantages can come from owning real estate or could be locked in by trading for cryptocurrency.

Cryptocurrency has more value risk than real estate (the price could drop by a larger amount and more quickly), but real estate may have more opportunity cost (the upside will be much more limited). The amount, type, and timing of the risks you are willing to assume will affect how you approach investing between real estate and cryptocurrency. And your overall experience with one side or the other may make you more comfortable with the investment type you already know.

If you don't already own real estate, it is probably premature to worry about loyalty or savings programs. If you do own real estate, you have many options. You can sell all or part your real estate for cryptocurrency. You could create a STO and tokenize the ownership of your real estate so that you are able to sell off part of it as your objectives dictate. If you have cryptocurrency and would like to lock in some of the appreciation you have received, trade it for real estate. Real estate transactions can improve liquidity of your crypto and may allow you to manage the capital gains you would have to pay if you sold it.

If you have funds to invest, all options are on the table. Do you get into real estate or crypto first? Do you invest in both? The fiat is very flexible but really should be moved into some sort of asset to stave off the inevitable depreciation that will make your money worth less the longer you hold it. Remember that having some fiat along with your real estate or your crypto can help to close deals.

Action Plan for Real Estate Investors

There are a few things that every real estate investor can do to begin working in cryptocurrency. First, take a few hundred dollars and buy some cryptocurrency. Buy some Bitcoin, Ether, REXNET or XTROPTIONS.GOLD. Get used to having a wallet and an address. Download the relevant apps for the crypto you decide to get. Learning the mechanics of buying, selling, trading, and sending crypto will make the process easier once you identify a deal you want to do.

If you already have a real estate business, brainstorm ways you could create a loyalty program or a savings program. Poll your customers to see if there is interest in paying with cryptocurrency. It may be that in your particular area or property type there is really no interest, but if the interest is there you have just found a competitive advantage.

Are you getting ready to sell your real estate? Think about your objectives in selling. Are you planning to buy a larger property? Are you planning to simplify your estate? Are you looking to diversify? You need to really understand your objectives in selling. Once you understand those, you can identify if any of the cryptocurrency approaches can meet them.

If you want to diversify but don't really want to sell, it may be that creating a STO and tokenizing your property so that you could sell part of it would be an attractive alternative. You will need to research STO companies to find one that can help you.

Action Plan for Cryptocurrency Investors

If you are a cryptocurrency investor and are wondering how to diversify into real estate, there are several actions you should take. The first is to get education about your preferred real estate property type and investments. Real estate is complex and there is a lot you need to know to evaluate a property for acquisition. You have to be able to read an income/expense report and a balance sheet and know what to expect for income and expense items for the type of real estate you are pursuing (hint: many sellers leave off important items like real estate taxes or management costs when they give you numbers).

Once you have some education or are working with a trusted advisor who can help you assess the real estate, you can look for properties that may be available in exchange for your cryptocurrency. This process can be more challenging than it looks. You usually need a sophisticated and experienced seller who can understand the advantages of accepting cryptocurrency for their property. Most real estate brokers have no idea how to construct a crypto for real estate deal. Working with more creative real estate agents like those at the National Council of Exchangors (including yours truly) can help. You will also need to prepare yourself to potentially qualify for a loan.

Alternatively, you might use your crypto experience to assist a real estate team in creating a STO in exchange for some amount of the STO tokens (ownership of the real estate). Cryptocurrency experience is frankly much more rare than real estate investing experience. What you already know can be an asset to someone else.

Wherever you are in your investing journey, do something. Take a step. Take a chance. Even a baby step can help you build momentum. The synergies between real estate and cryptocurrency are profound and too profitable to ignore. If you get stuck, reach out. I'm always here. And when you succeed, I would love it if you let me know. Success breeds success.

Move forward.

AFTERWORD

W HEN THE IDEA FOR this book first began to germinate, I thought it was going to be a book about buying real estate with cryptocurrency. That was how I originally combined real estate and crypto, and it seemed to me that it was an important topic. So many in cryptocurrency were focused on white papers and crypto exchanges. I thought that actually using cryptocurrency for something real would be a novel approach that would engage cryptocurrency investors and real estate investors alike. I also found no one else looking at barter tokens. Barter tokens are such an interesting approach, but it is an approach that doesn't fit well with other cryptocurrencies (but is ideal for real estate).

As I began researching, however, I saw many other intersections between real estate and crypto. Property tokenization was such a cool idea. I looked into creating a tokenization for an assisted living purchase I was working on. But I ran into issue after issue. Every company I talked to seemed to have too narrow a focus to make the effort worthwhile. And many of the best ones wouldn't handle a tokenization within the U.S. because they weren't licensed broker-dealers and didn't believe they could legally issue tokens in the U.S.

I kept researching and found idea after idea for combining real estate and crypto. And many of the ideas were synergistic. Gradually, the book took shape as a way of exploring three transformations:

deal-making, ownership, and management. These unifying themes helped pull the book together and improved the flow and synergy of the ideas.

When I was completing my first draft, Bitcoin had jumped from around $3,500 to over $15,000. But as I am completing the book, Bitcoin has crossed the $50,000 mark and speculators are talking about $100,000 by the end of the year. Of course, others say Bitcoin prices will retrench and Bitcoin will lose half its value. These are exactly the same discussions we had in 2017 as Bitcoin reached $20,000 for the first time. No one knows what will happen.

But the idea of cryptocurrency and blockchain, a trustless, immutable system for managing transactions, has created new hope for a world currency. Almost every country is planning a national coin on a blockchain. And payment services like PayPal and MasterCard are rolling out payment methods (both sending and receiving) that will integrate the top few cryptocurrencies into the world payment systems.

When the environment is changing so fast, it is hard to decide when to cut it off, publish the book, and fix (at least in electrons and paper) the ideas. But here we are. I think there are ideas in the book that are still emerging. I don't know if they will ultimately look the way I envision. I'm likely to be wrong, or others are likely to innovate in directions I had never considered. Perhaps in a year or two as I continue my own investment approaches and coordinate with others, there will be advanced techniques that will justify a sequel (or an update).

Thank you for making it all the way through the book. If you have gotten this far, I suspect you are as interested as I am in how cryptocurrency and real estate work together. Going forward, I will be gathering additional material and publishing a monthly news-letter on topics of cryptocurrency and real estate. Considering how fast things are evolving, there will be no shortage of topics! You can engage with me at https://CryptoREBook.com if you are interested in finding out more about cryptocurrency and real estate and staying current with the newest techniques and opportunities. And you will be the first to know if a sequel or updated version is in the works. I look forward to collaborating with you as we create the future of cryptocurrency and real estate.

ABOUT THE AUTHOR

STEVE STREETMAN is a data scientist, systems engineer, commercial real estate investor and exchangor, and an avid cryptocurrency investor. His background in cryptography and long career in systems integration and risk assessment combined with real estate investment expertise means that he is uniquely placed to combine cryptocurrency and real estate.

Steve has written numerous articles for real estate investment magazines and regularly presents at his local real estate investment association. He teaches the commercial investing course at the DCREIA. Steve is a member of the National Association of Realtors (NAR) and the National Council of Exchangors (NCE).

Steve lives in Maryland, USA, with his wife, Christy. They have two children, Michael and Holly. When not constructing investment deals or applying advanced algorithms to important problems, Steve enjoys sailing, tennis, music, and theater.